ABSTRACT IMAGINATIONS

Adult Coloring Book

Volume 1

Featuring
Original Artwork by

Dawn V. Taylor

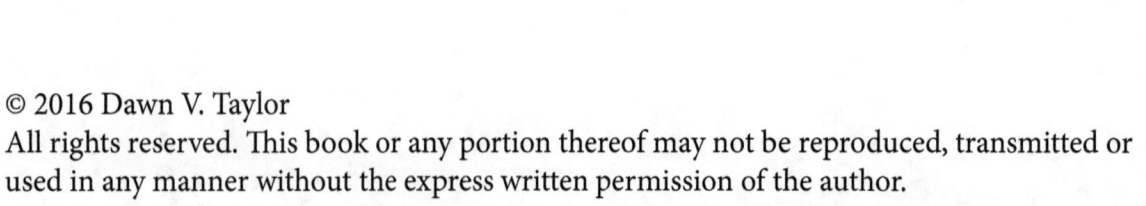

I have been drawing ever since I was able to hold my first crayon. Since then, I was encouraged to share my drawings, so a coloring book was born. I'd like to thank my family for supporting me, especially my husband Richard, my friends for inspiring me (Sandy, Sandy Gail and Leanne), and my art teacher, Mr. Art Harrington, for encouraging me many years ago. Thank you little brother Mark Viola for assisting me in realizing my dream and thank you Feebee Houck and Amelia Ross for assisting with photography.

All the drawings are my own crazy and abstract creations, a way of destressing. I used to color them myself, now I am sharing them with you to color! I hope you enjoy coloring them as much as I did creating them.

For limited edition prints or other coloring products, you can visit my website at www.dawnvtaylorart.com. Never be afraid to create, even if you think what you create is weird!

Dawn Viola Taylor

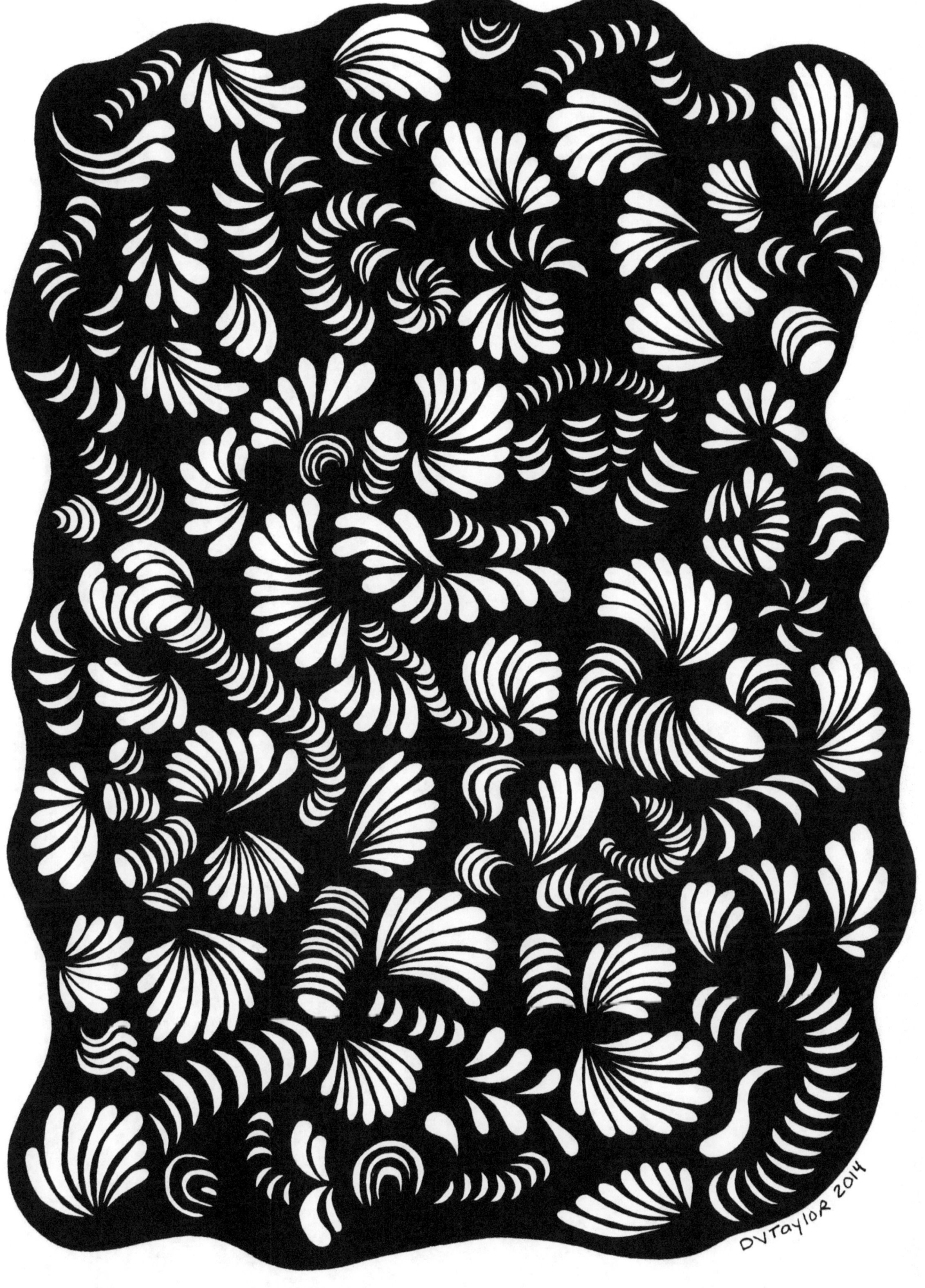

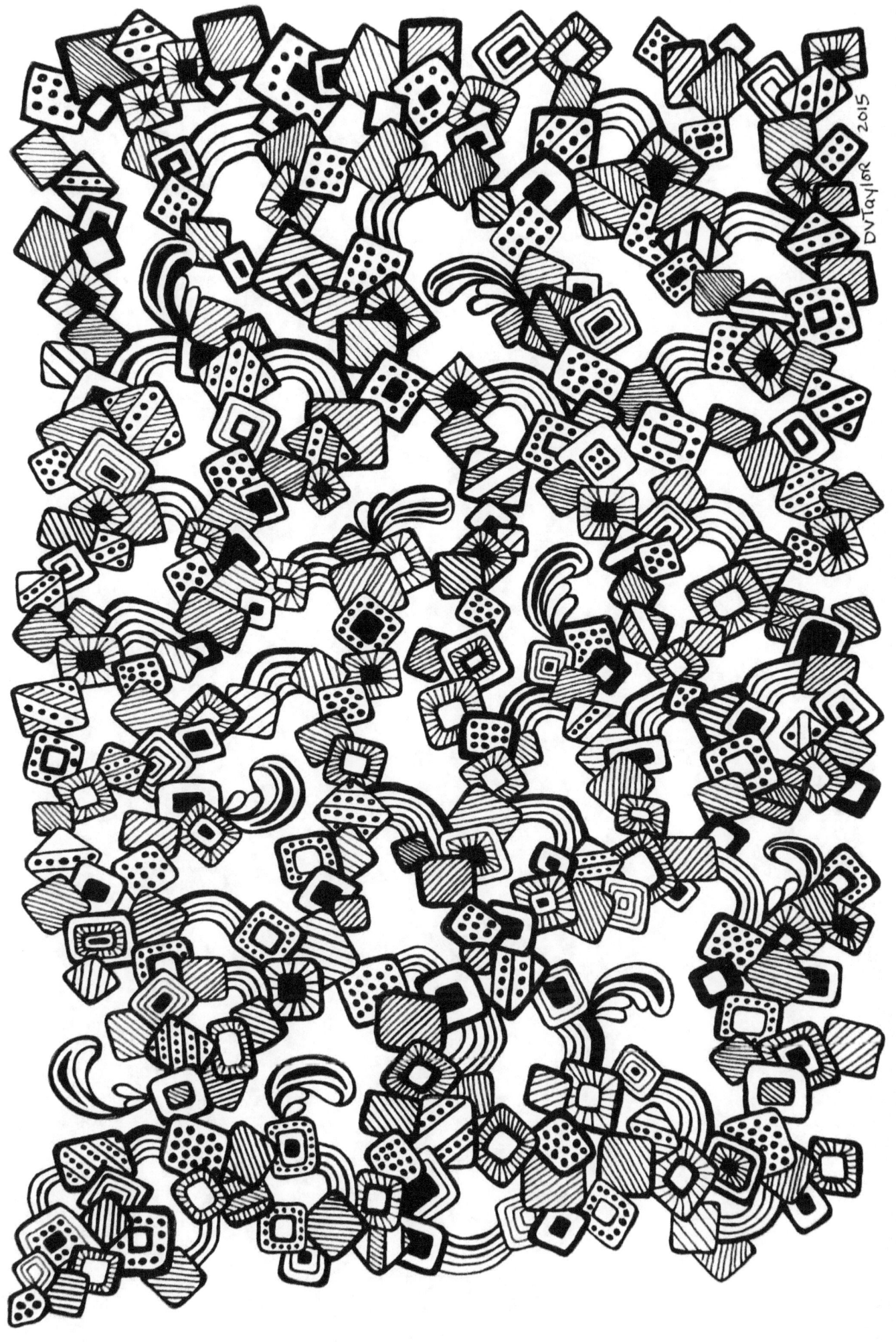

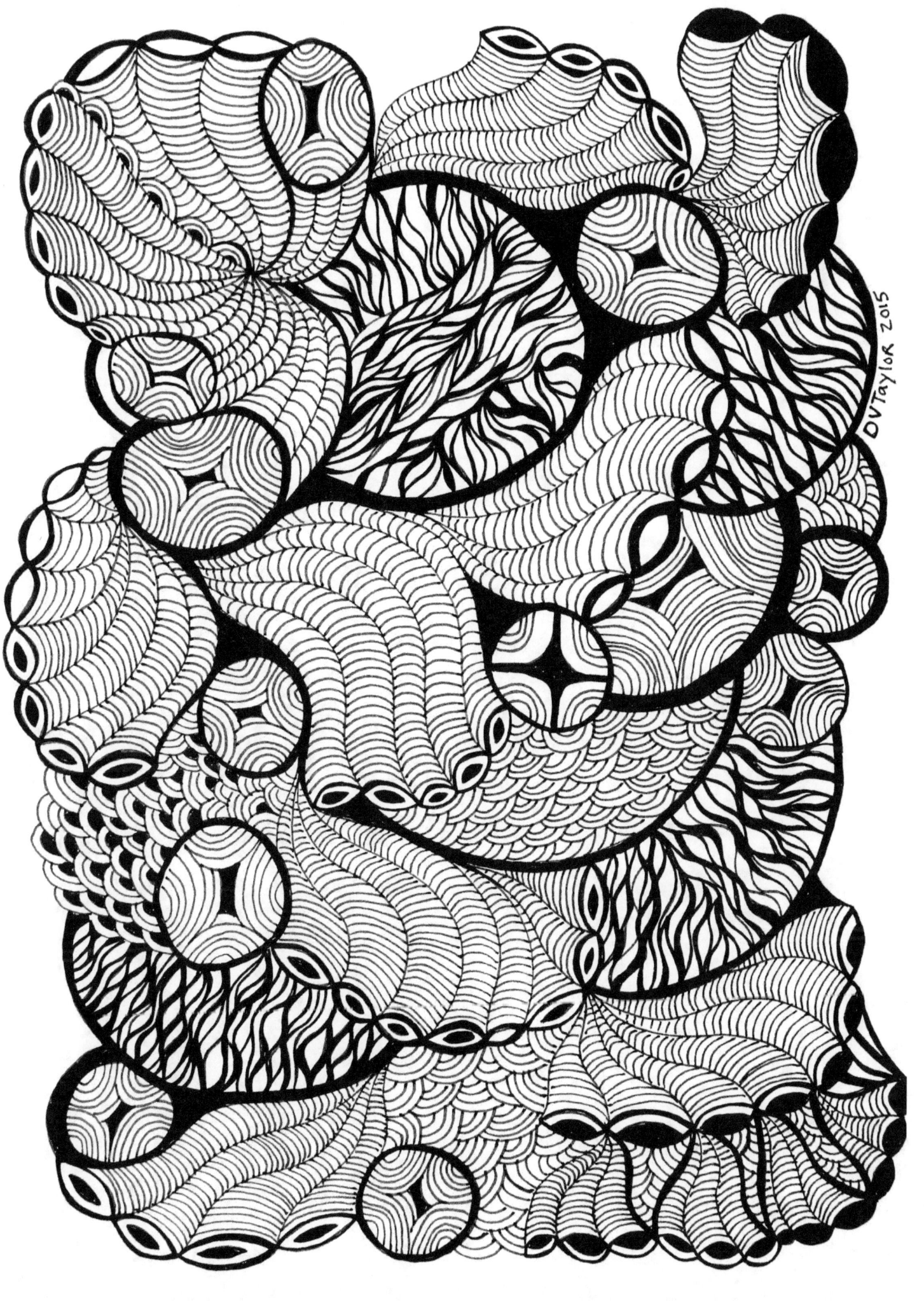

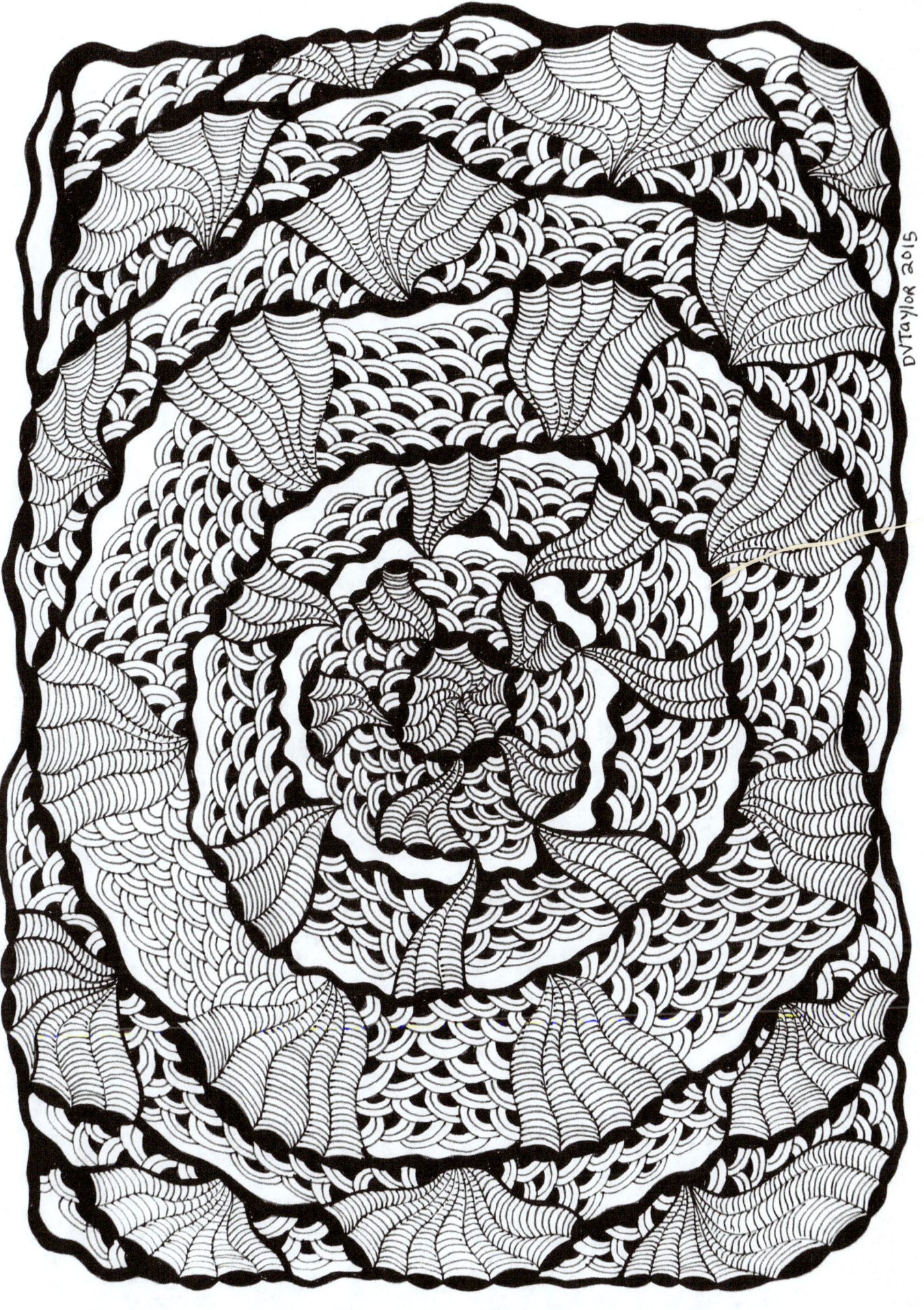

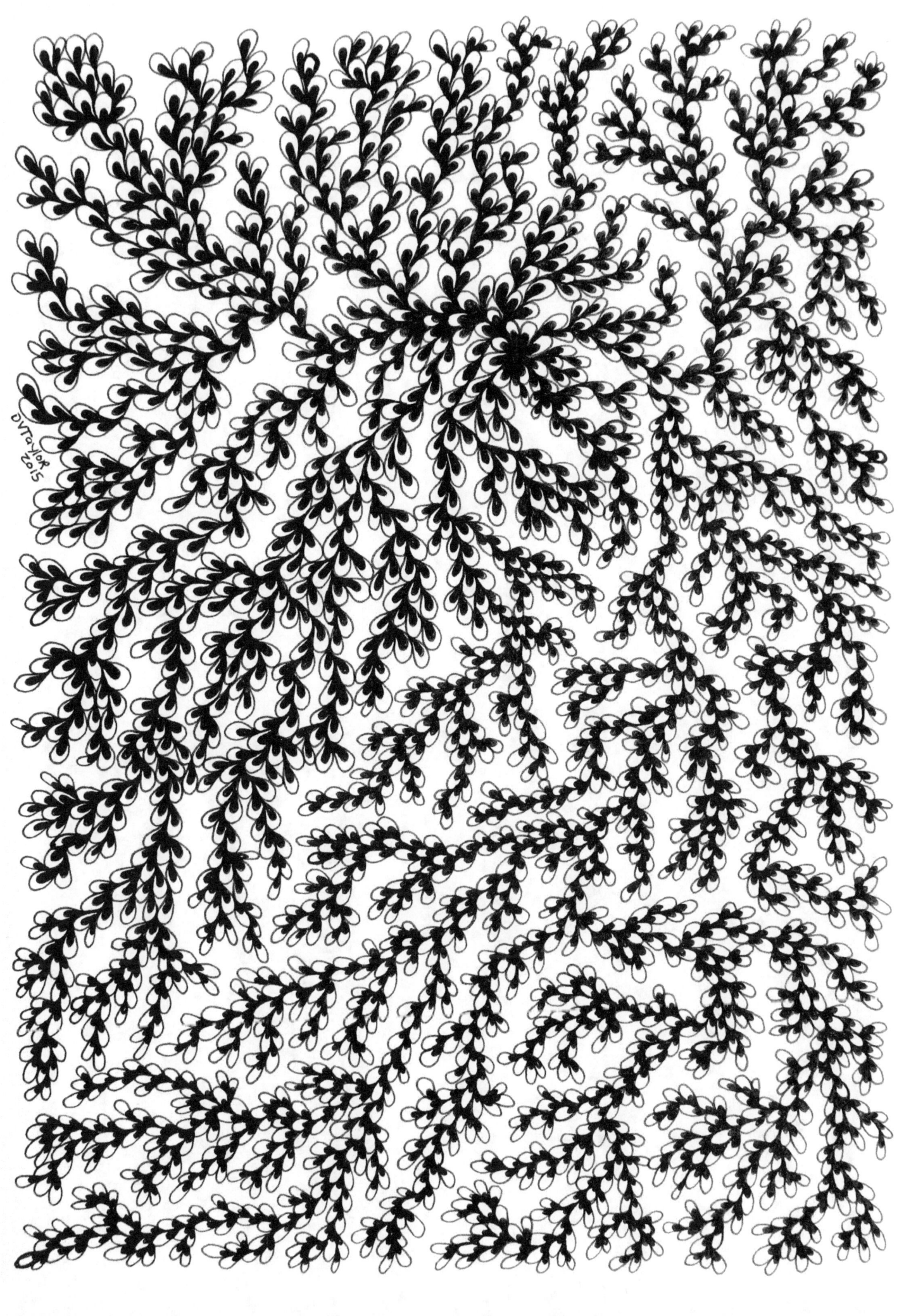

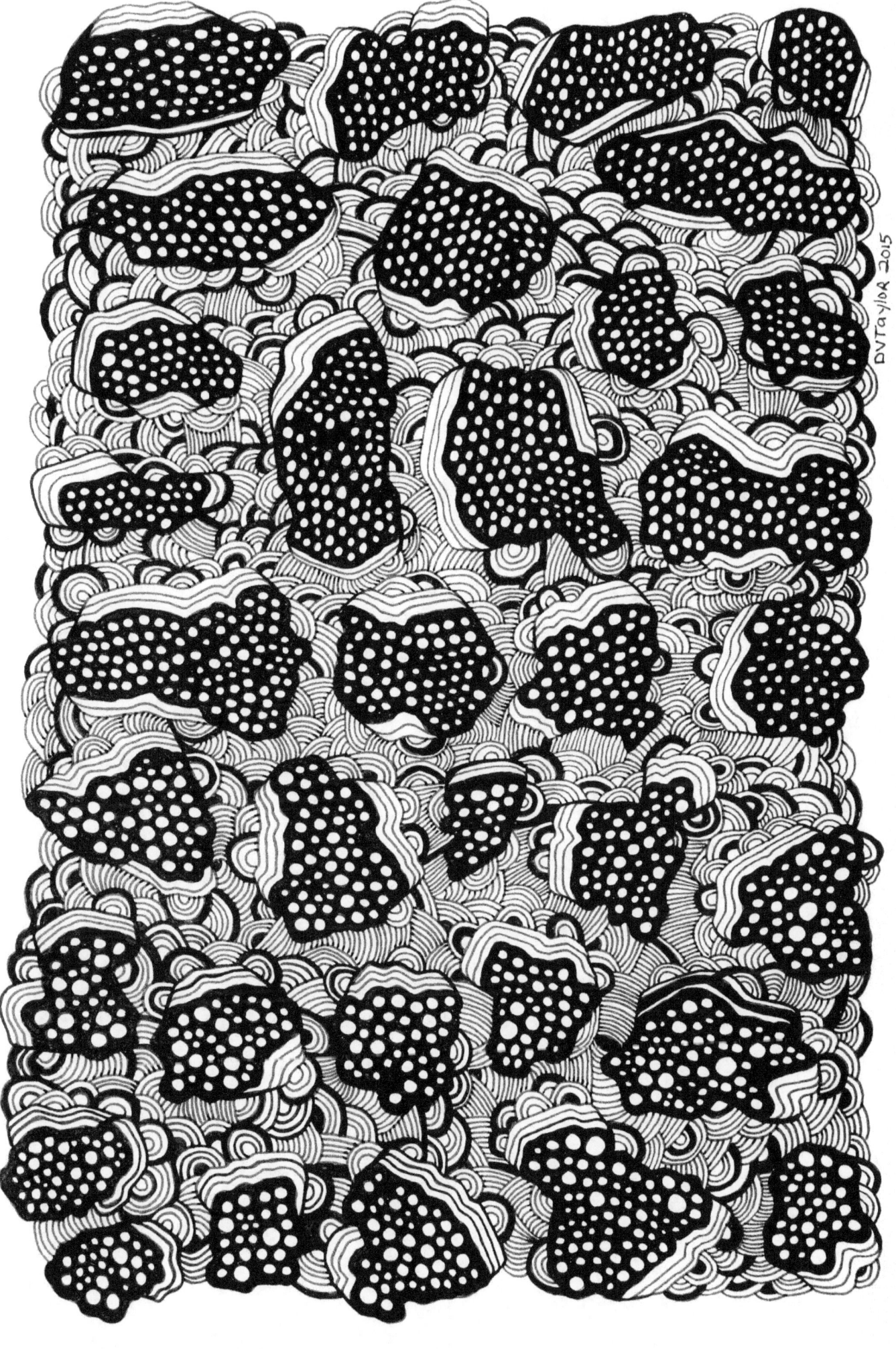

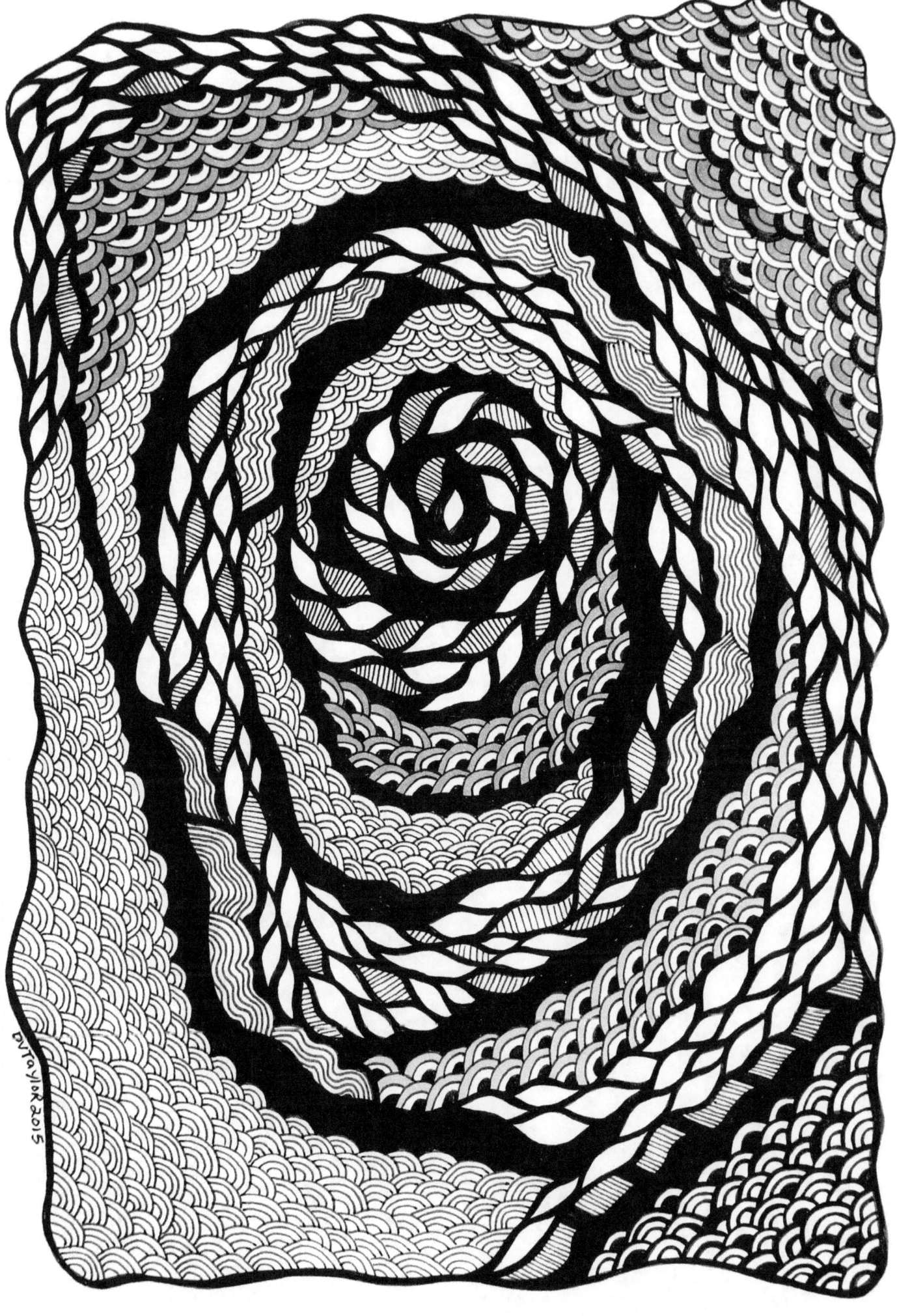

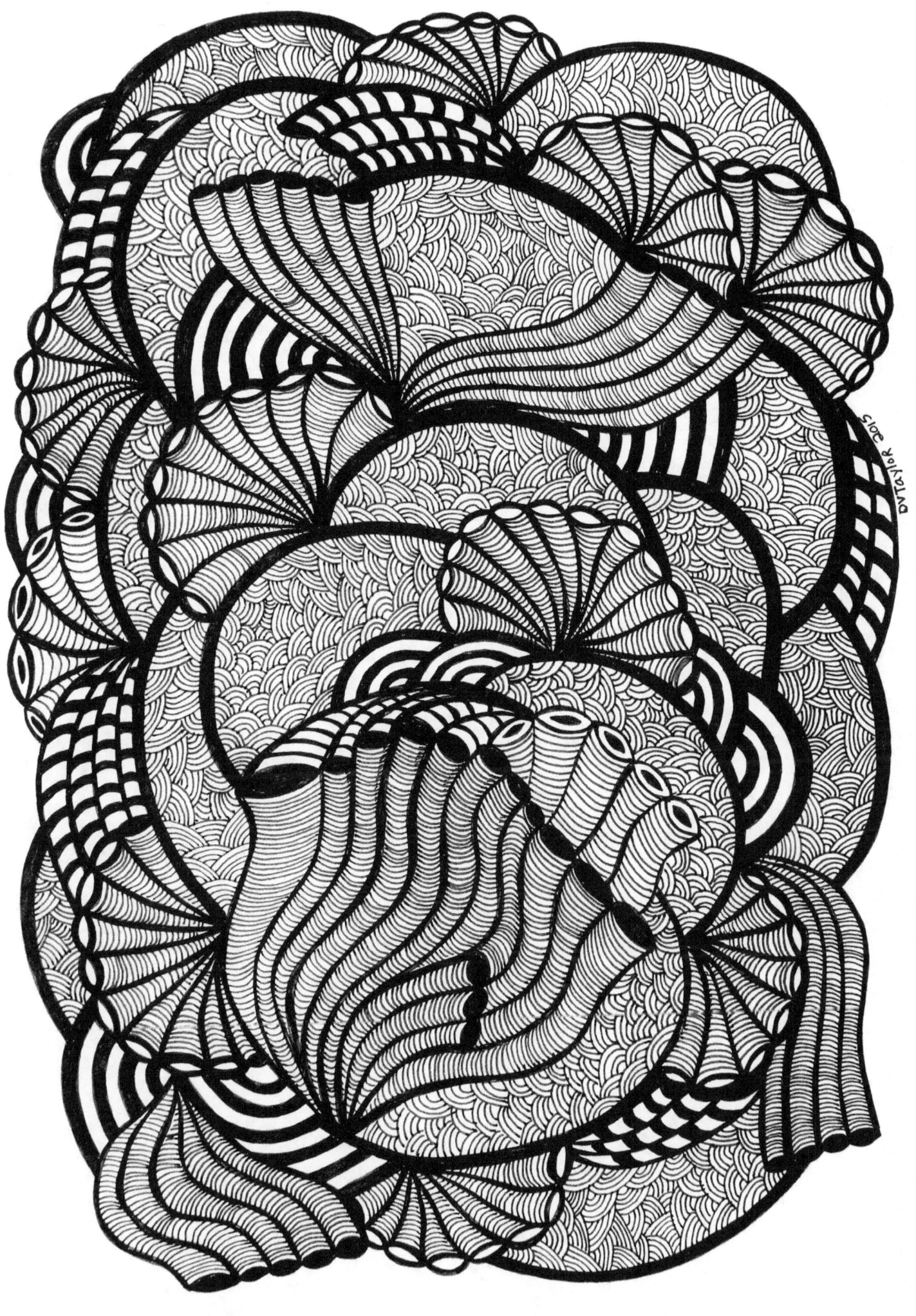

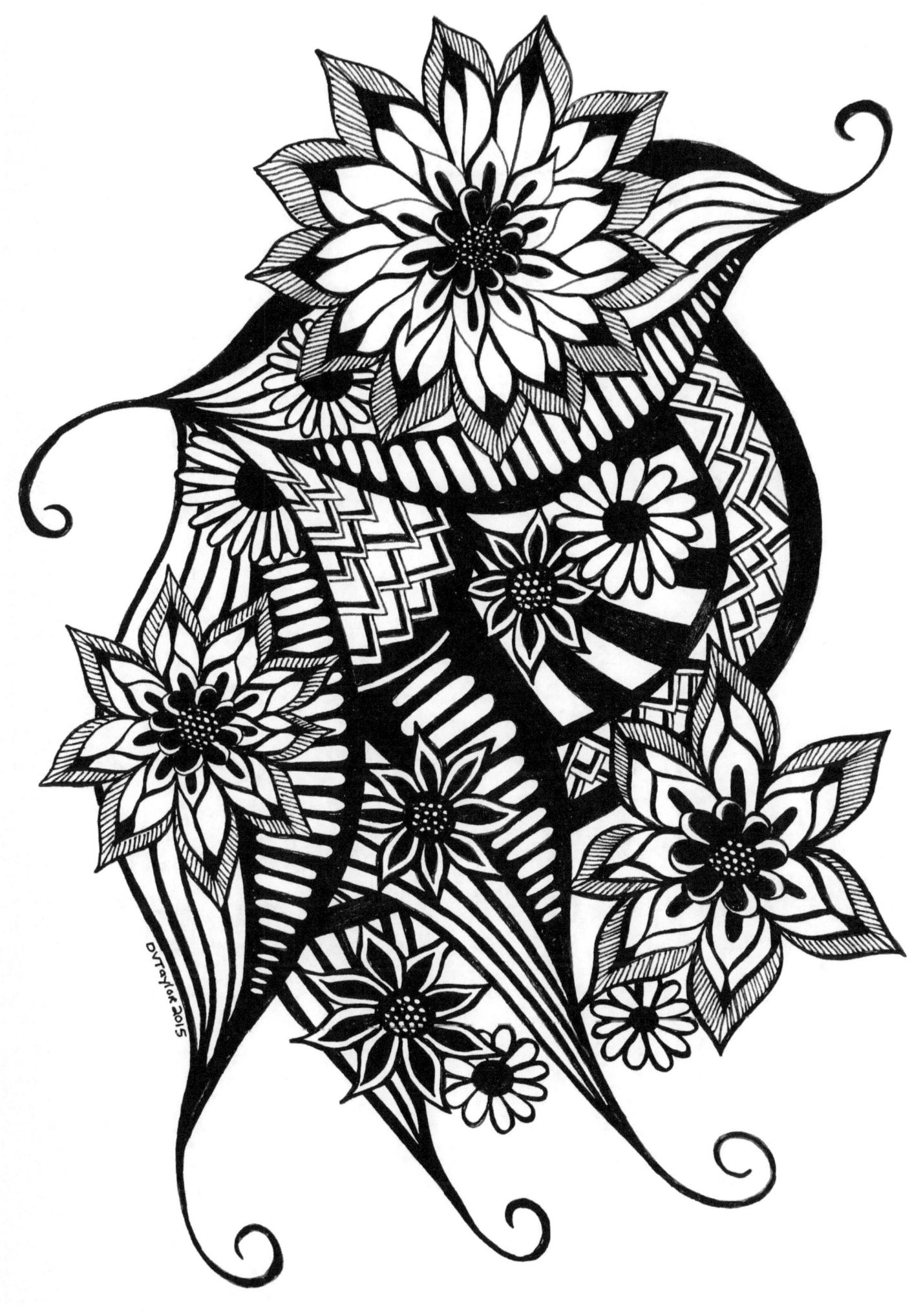

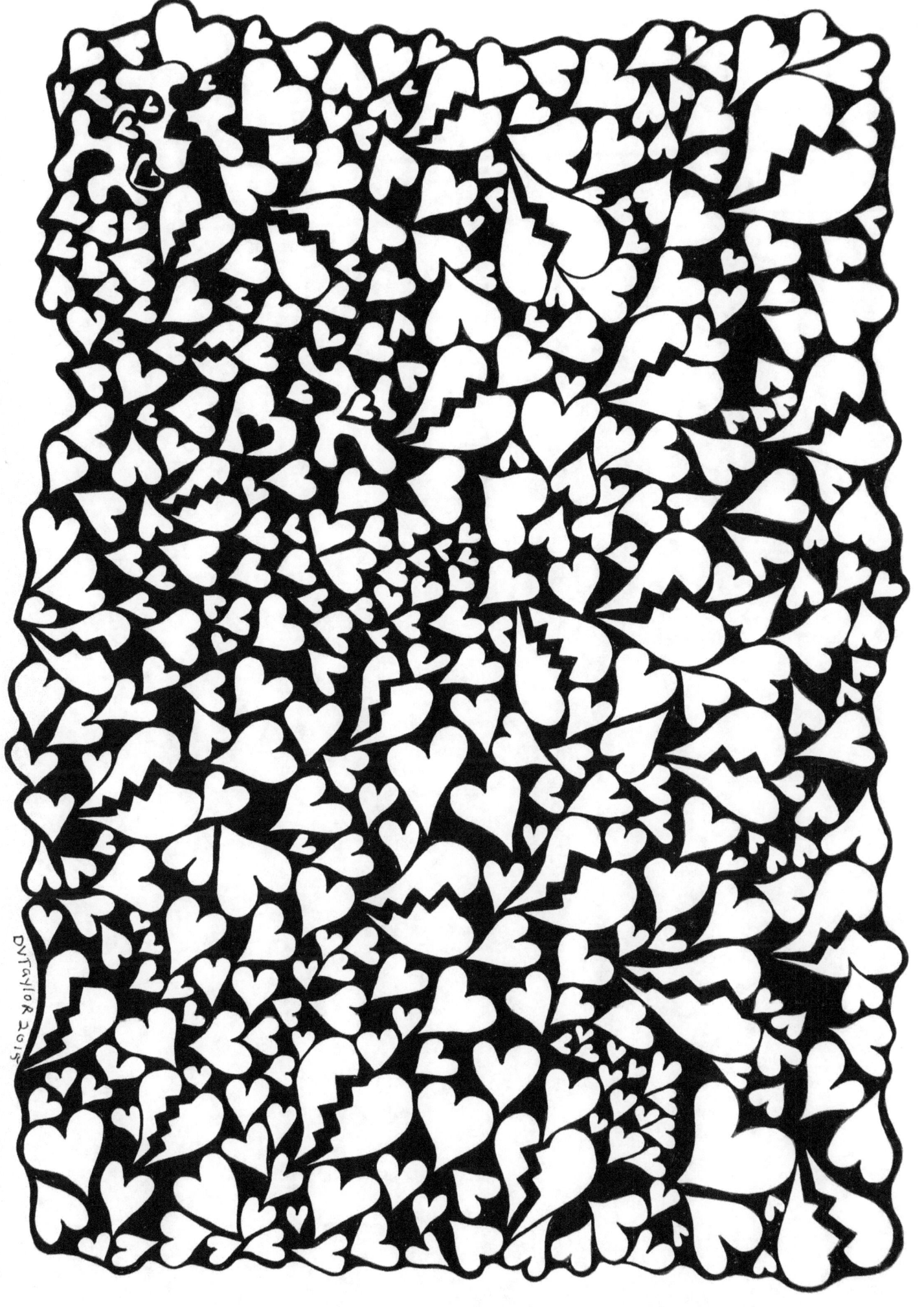

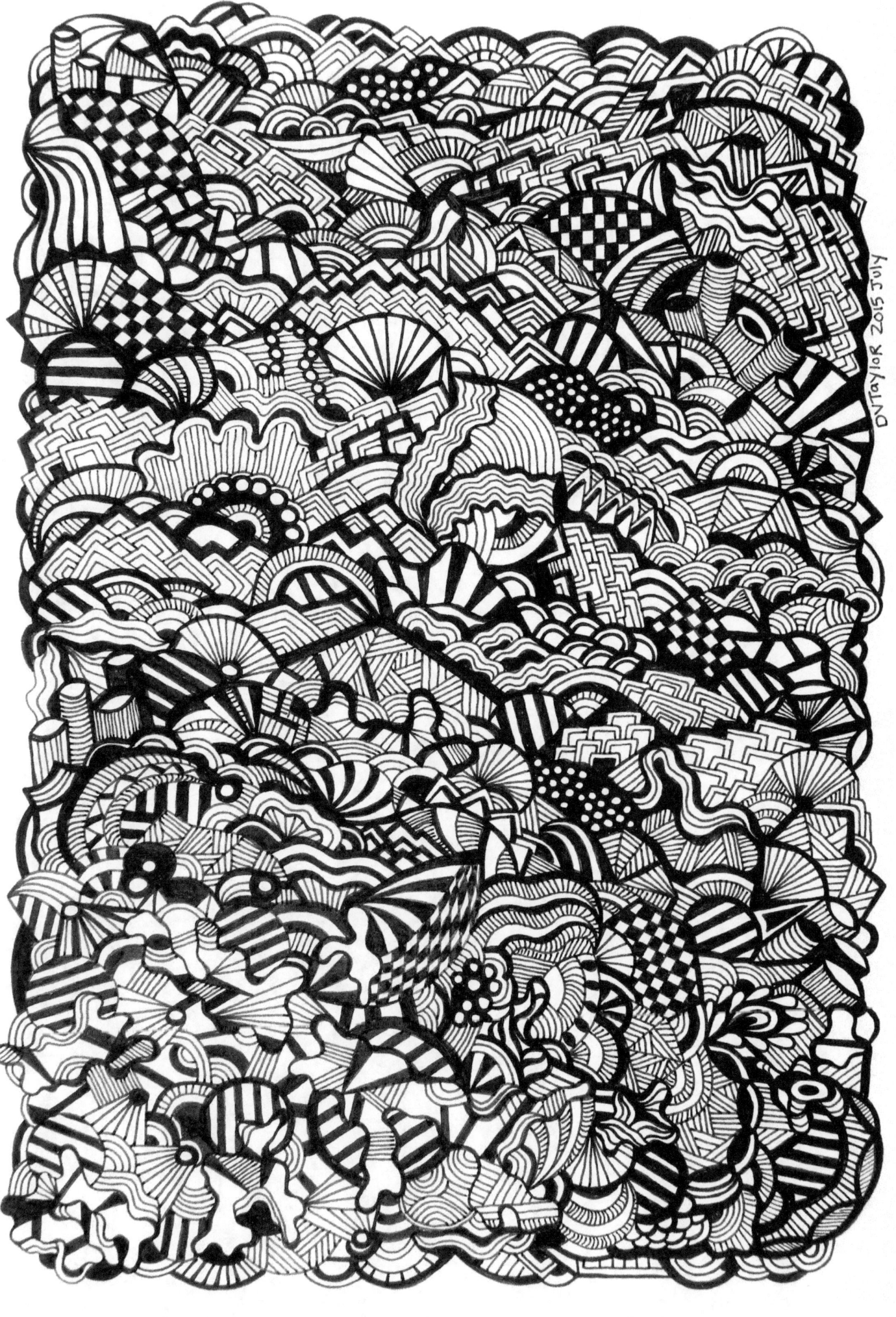

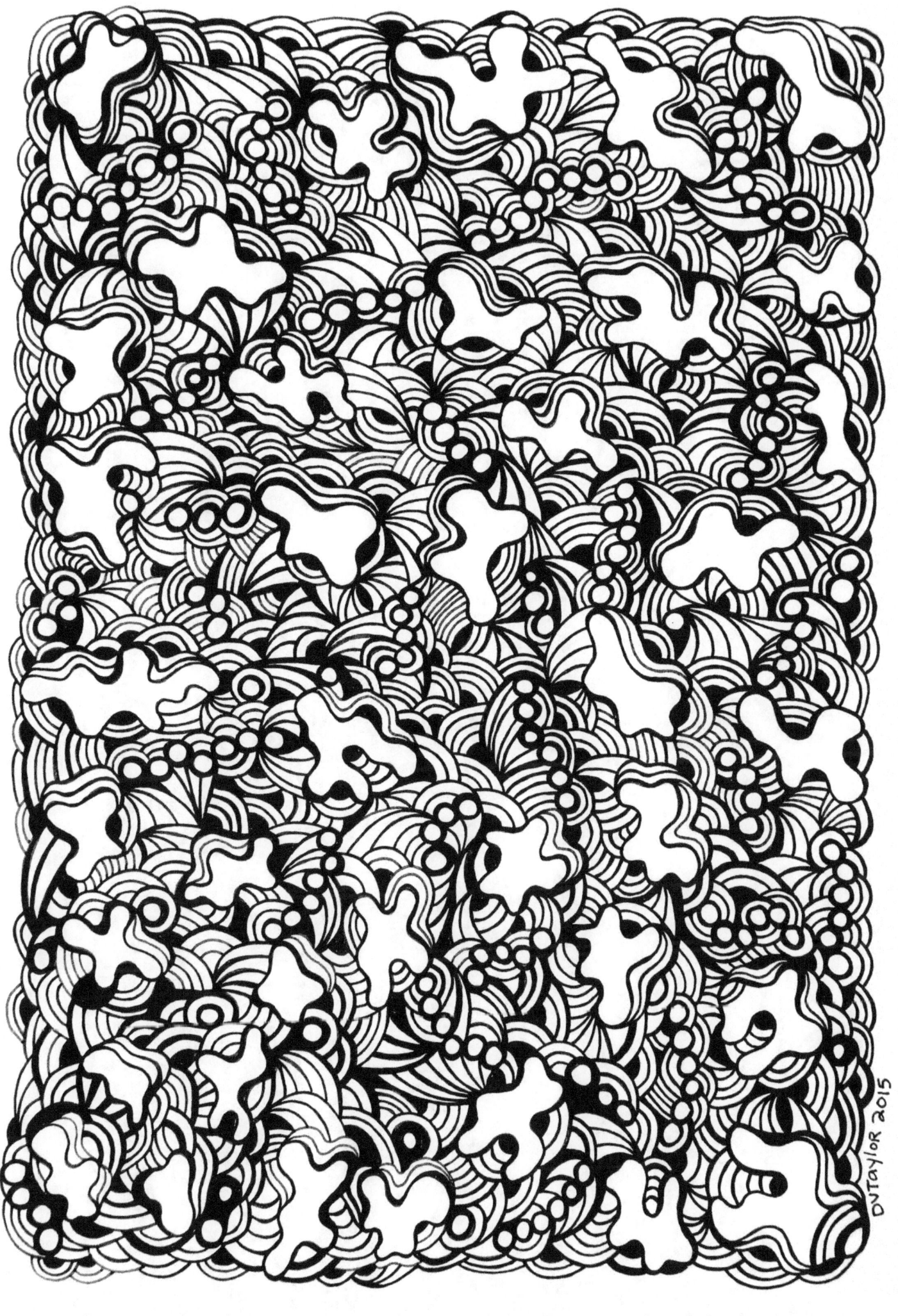

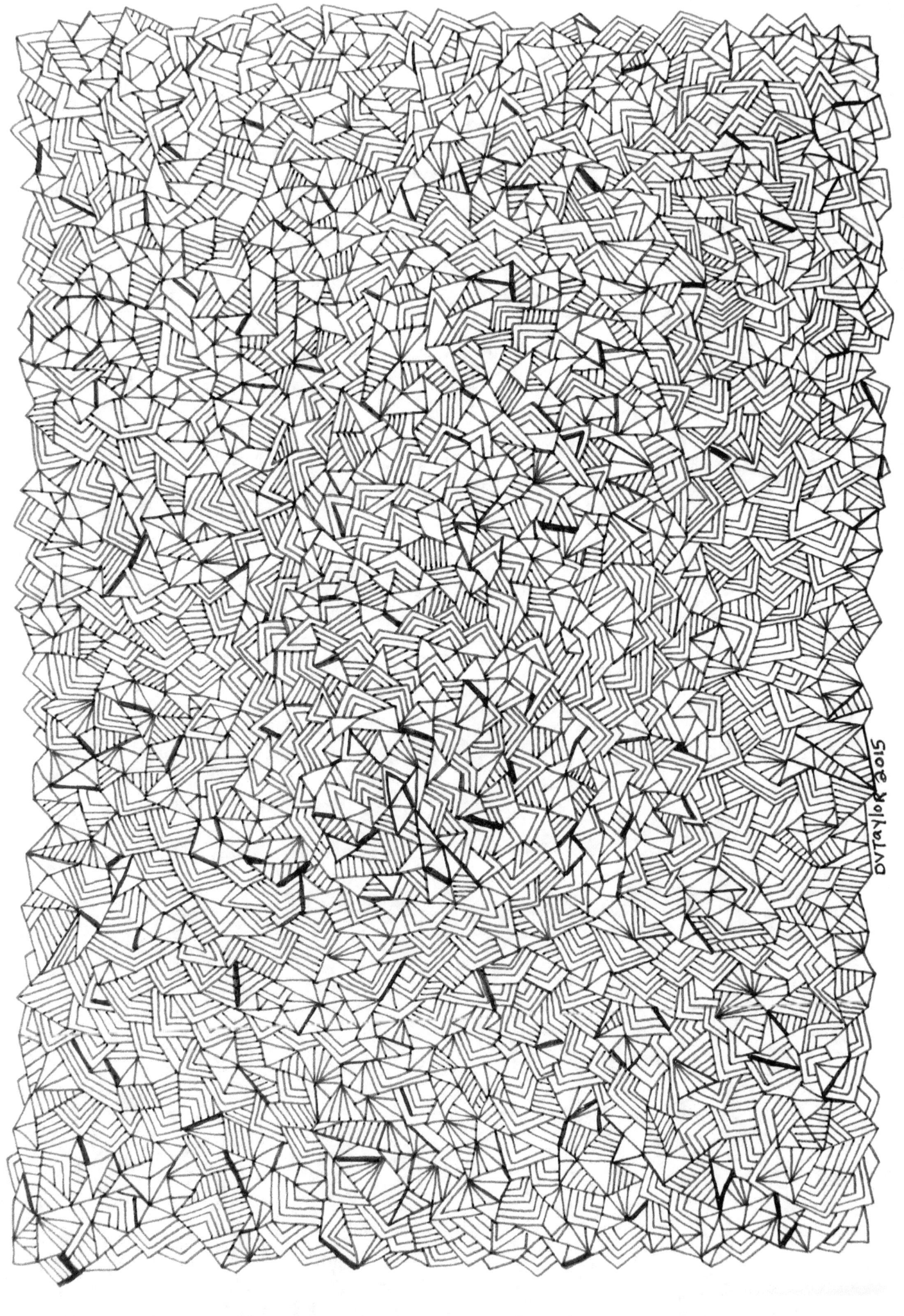

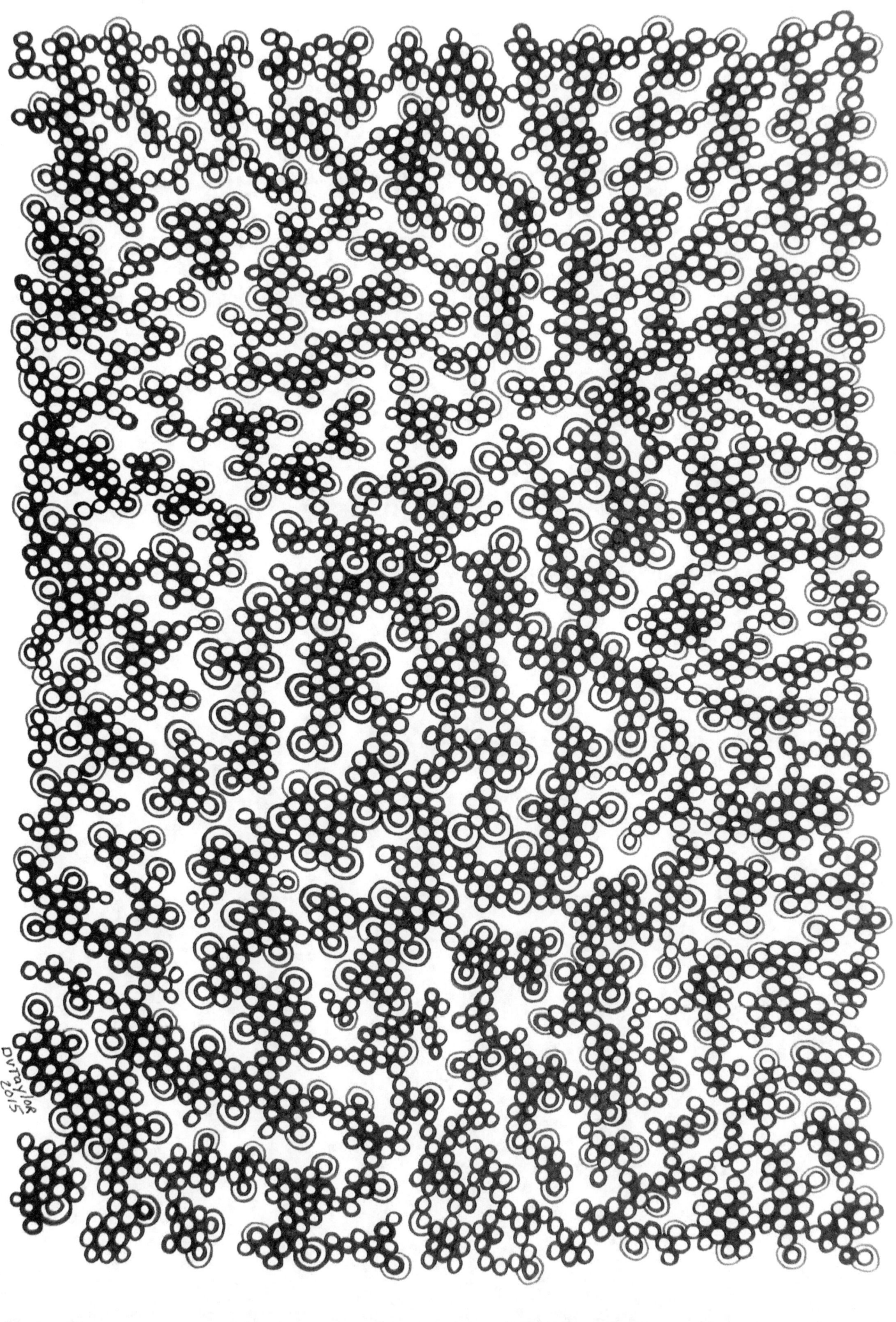

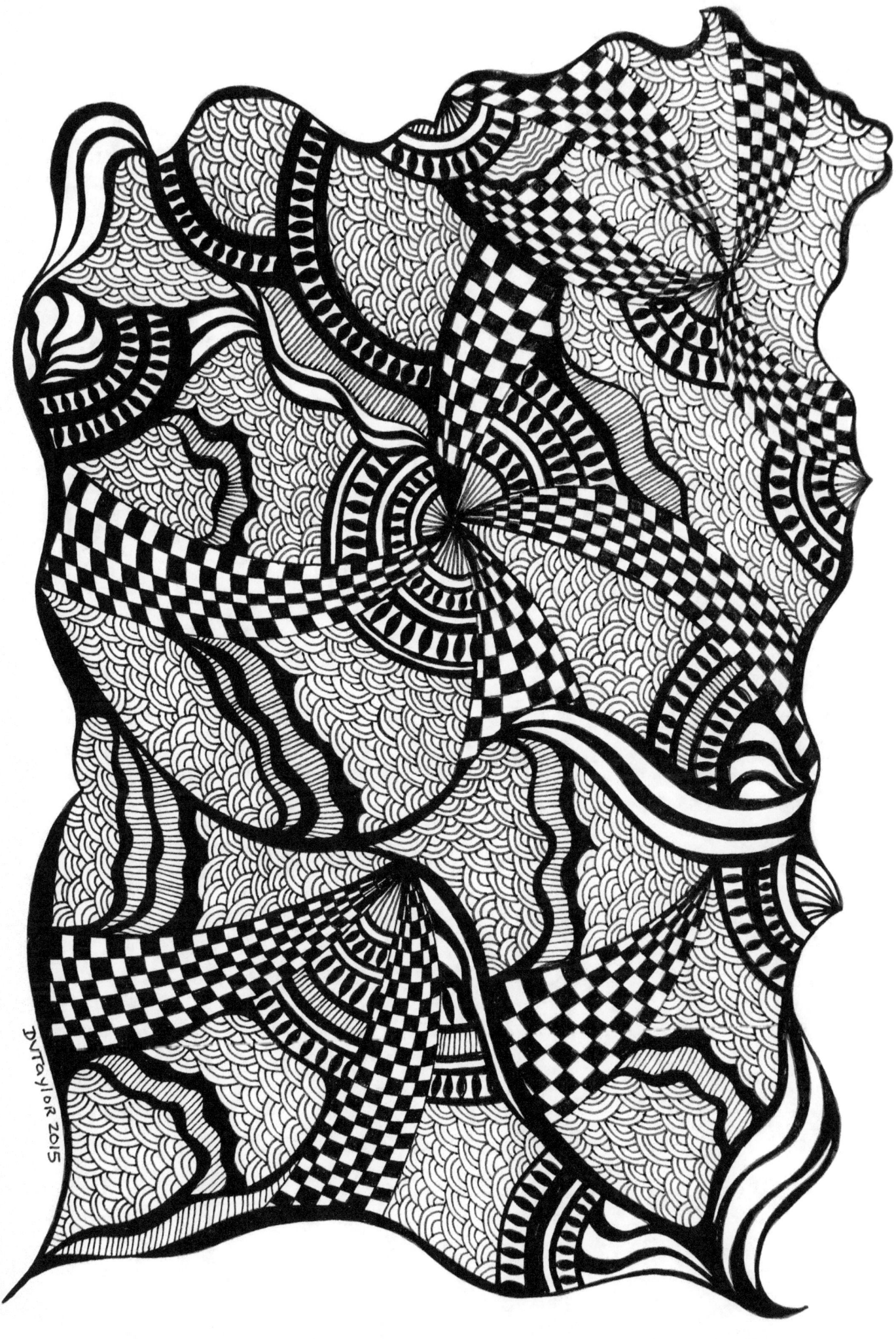

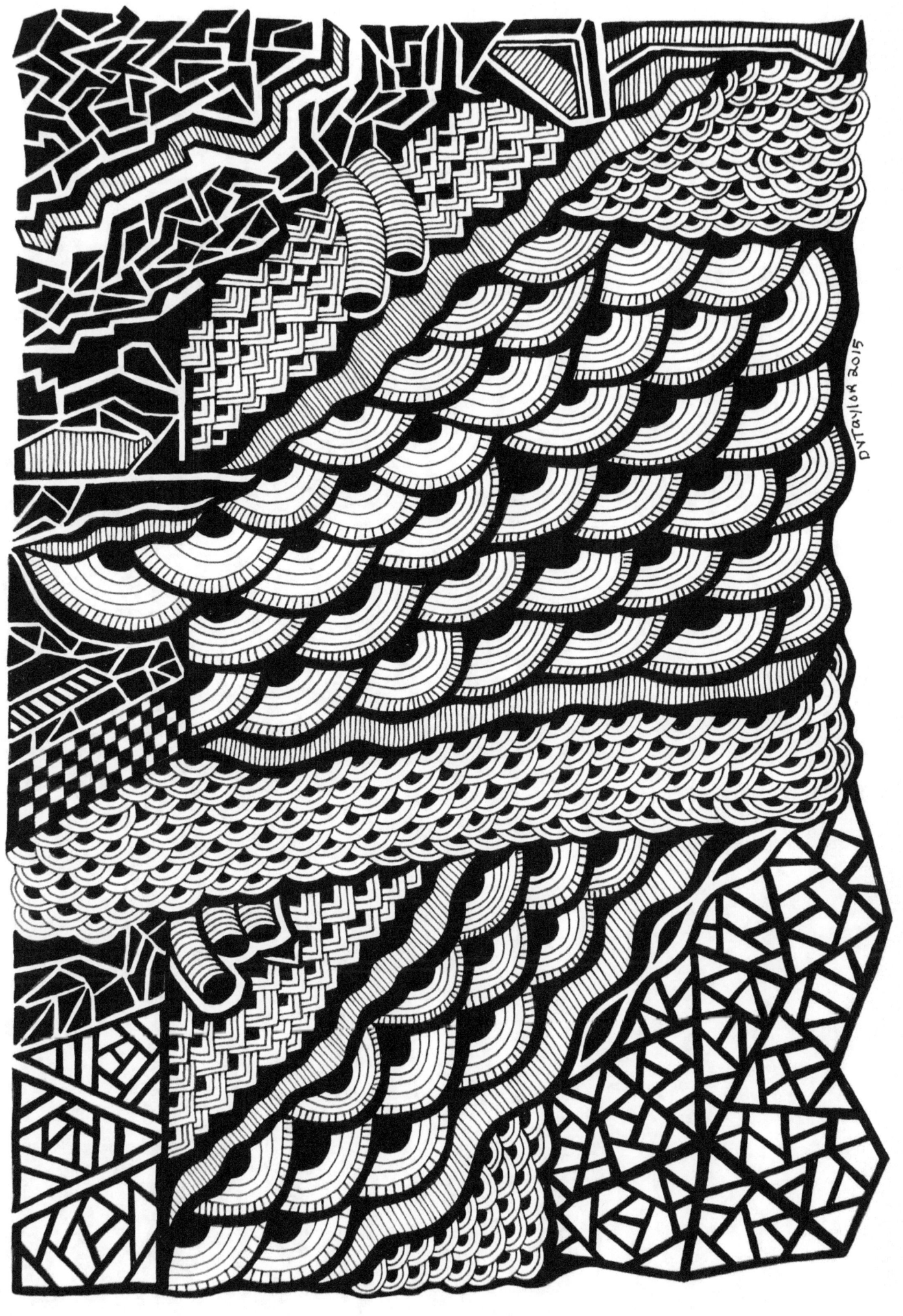

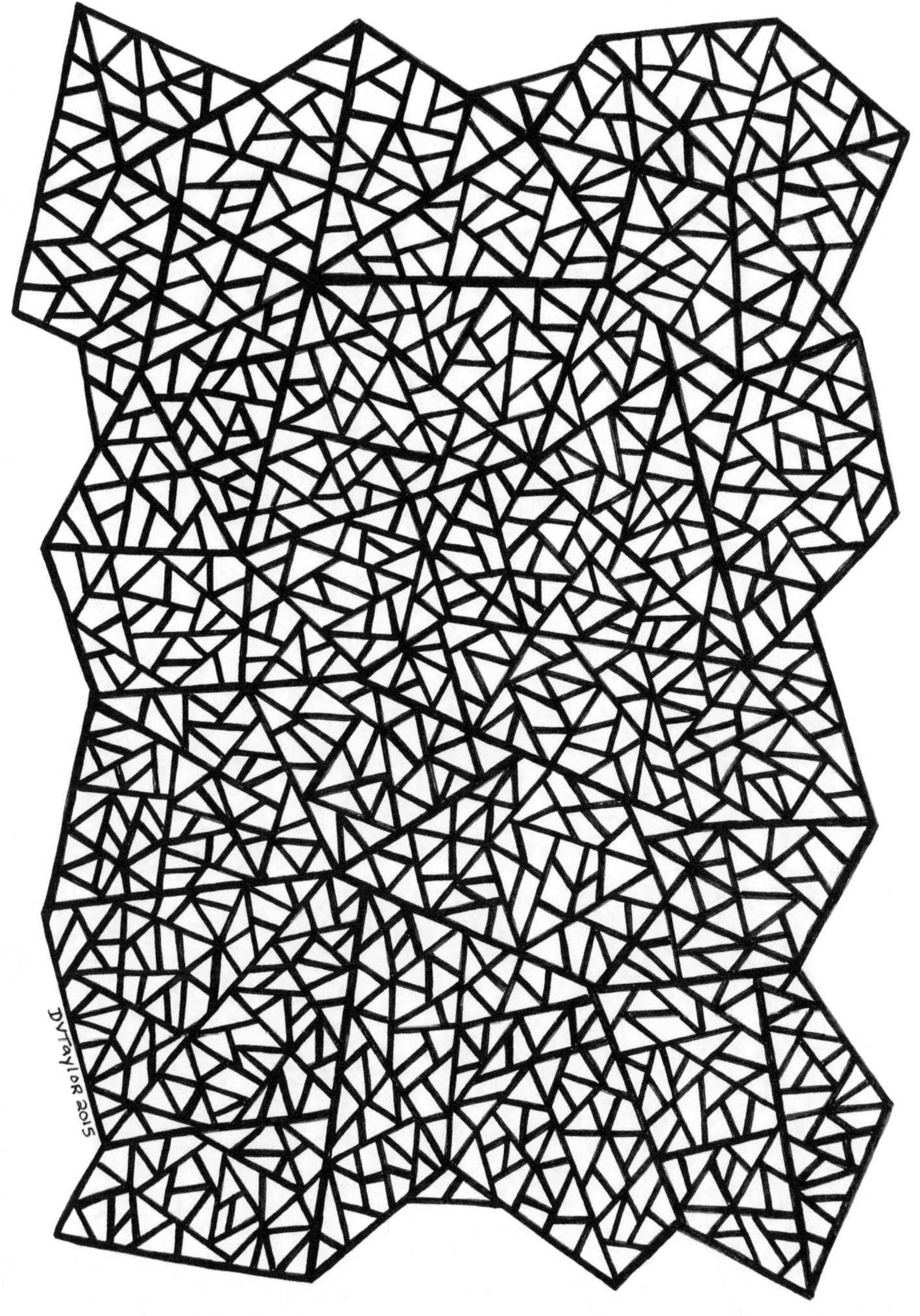

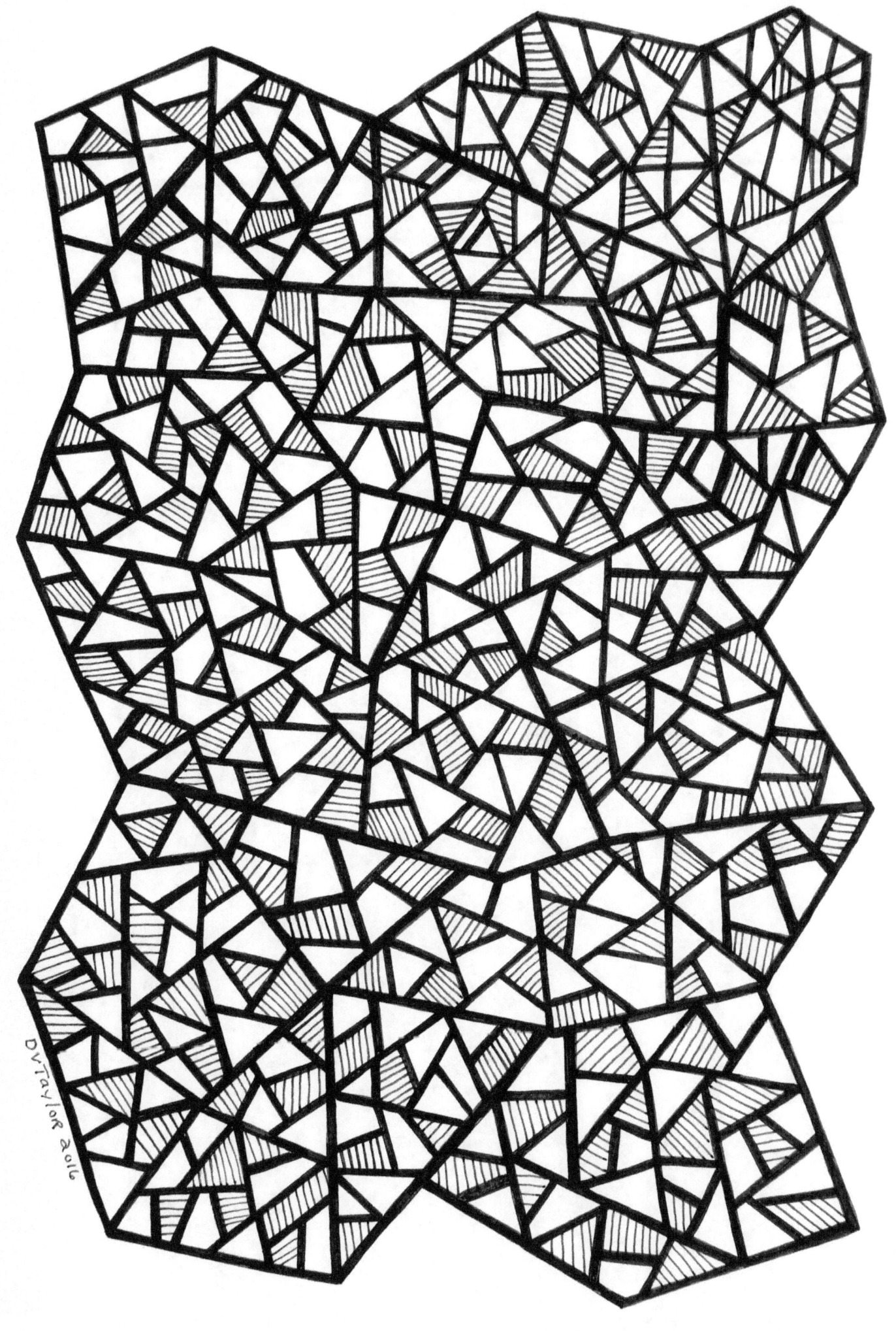

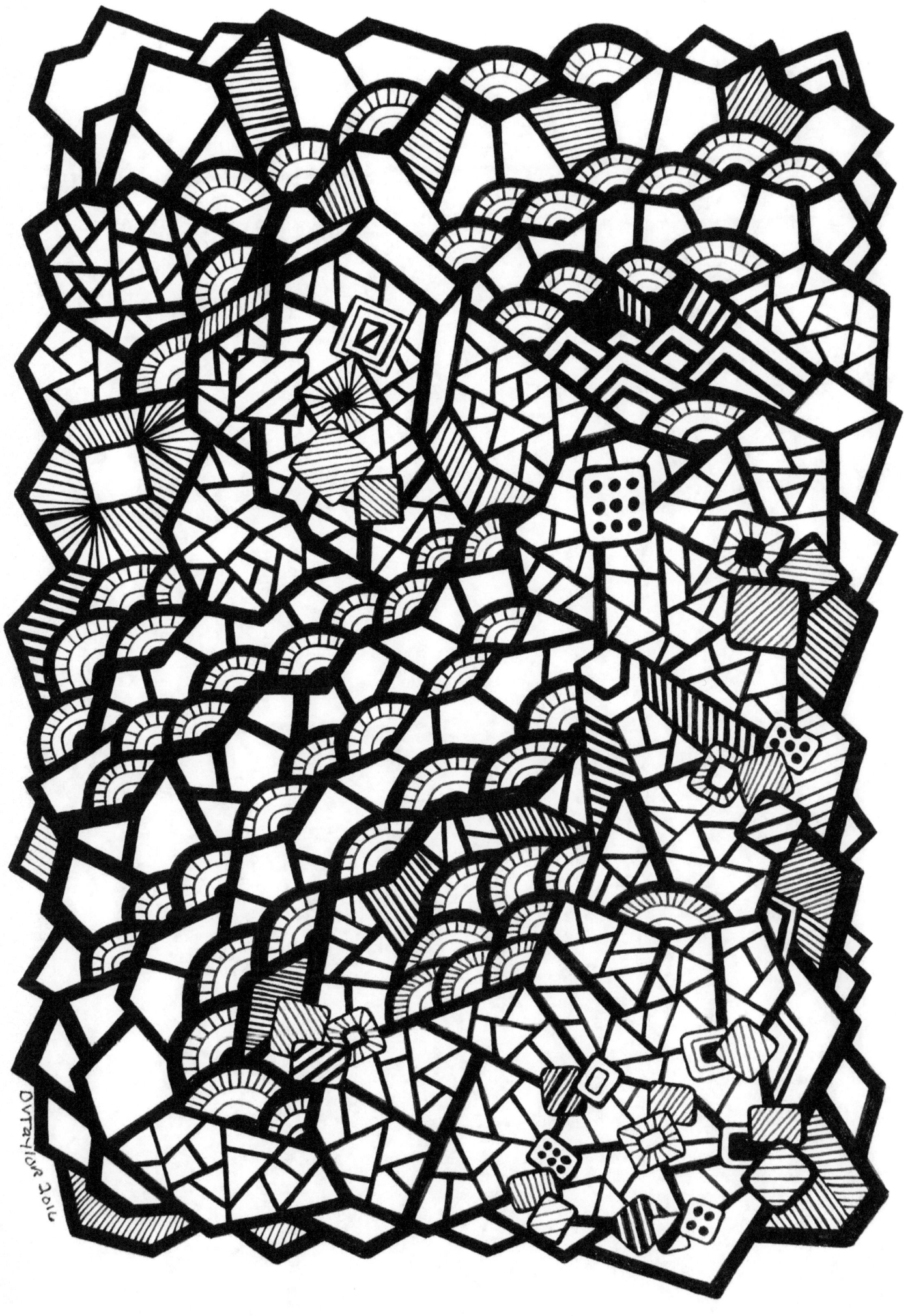

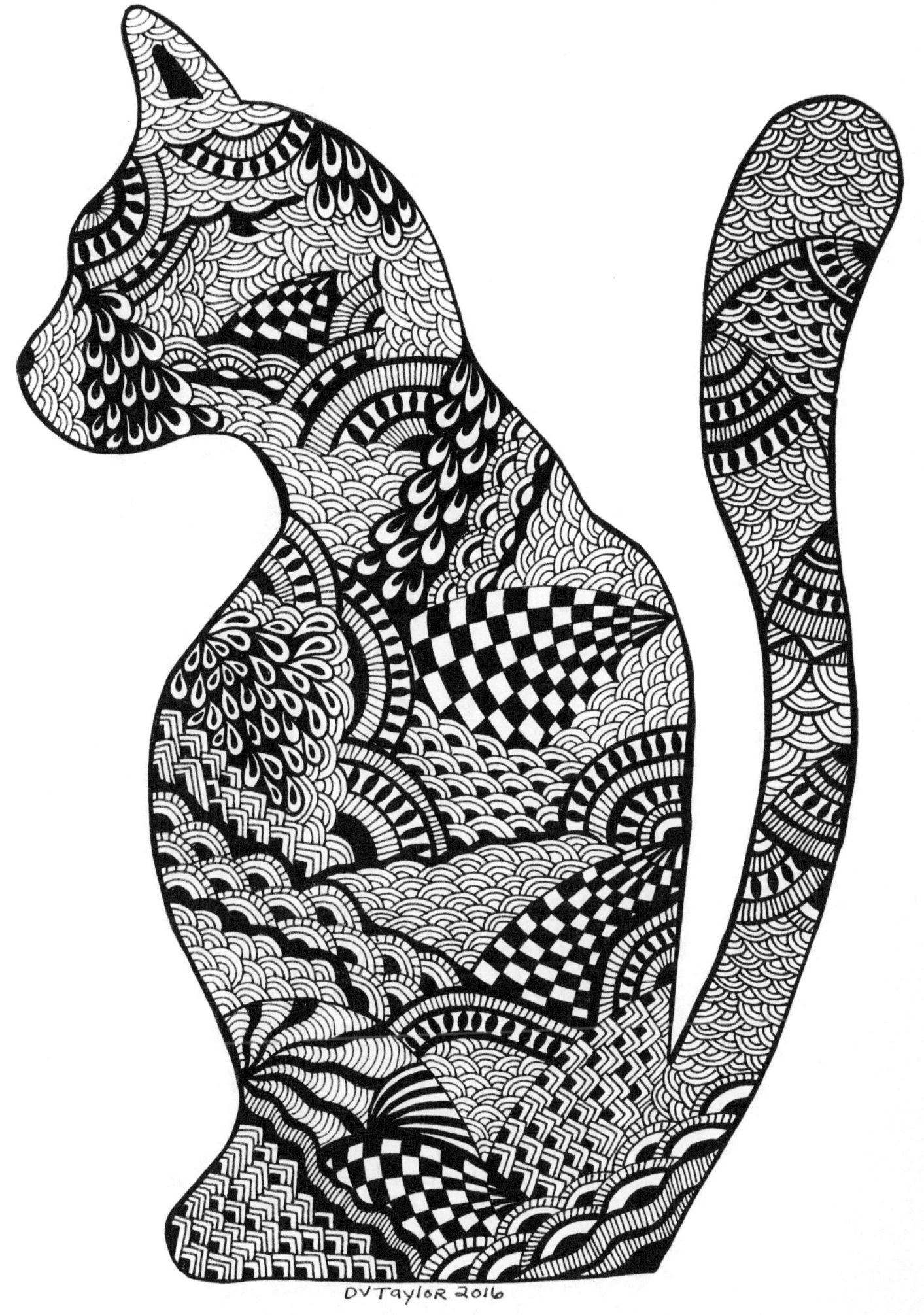

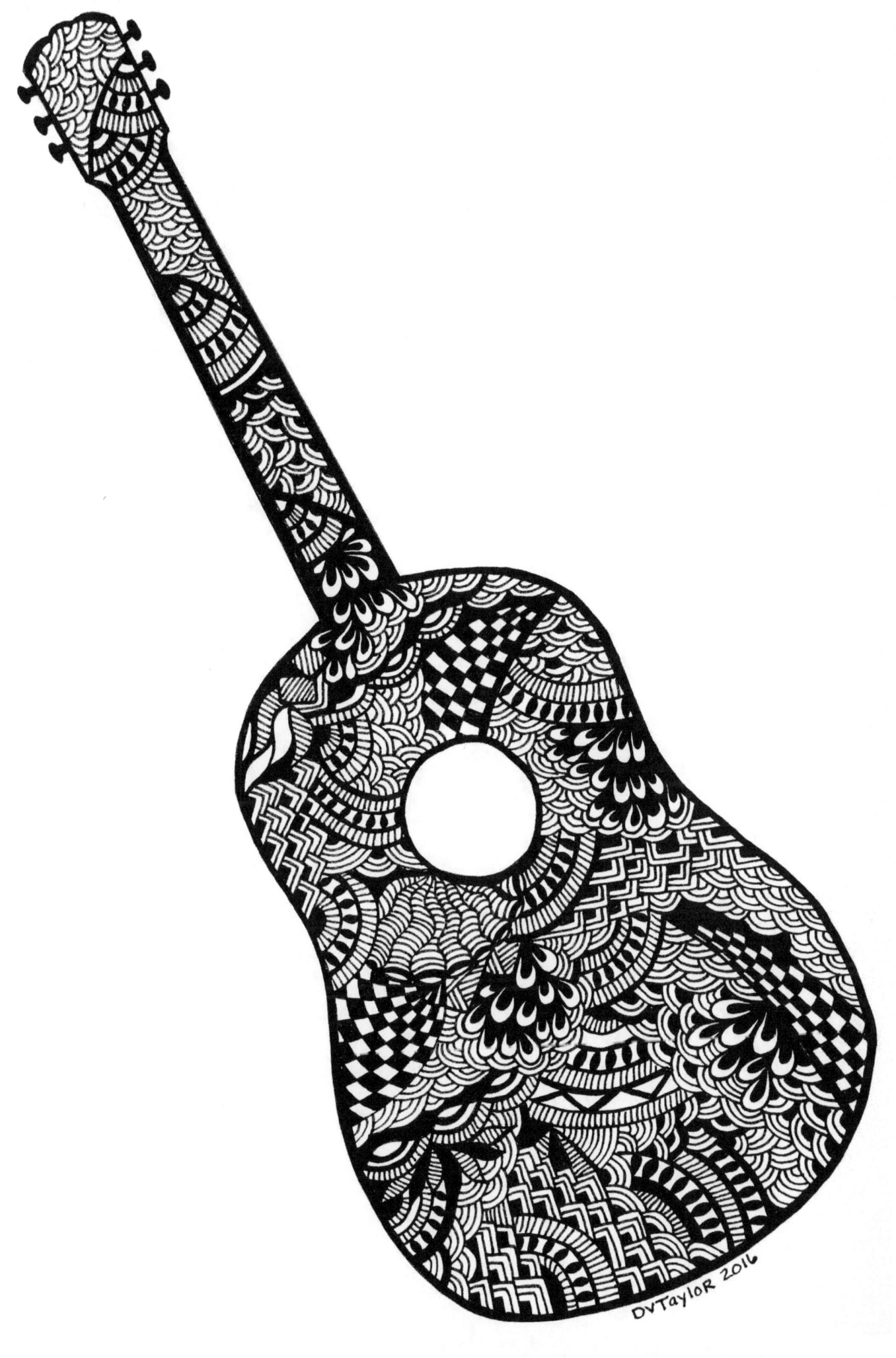

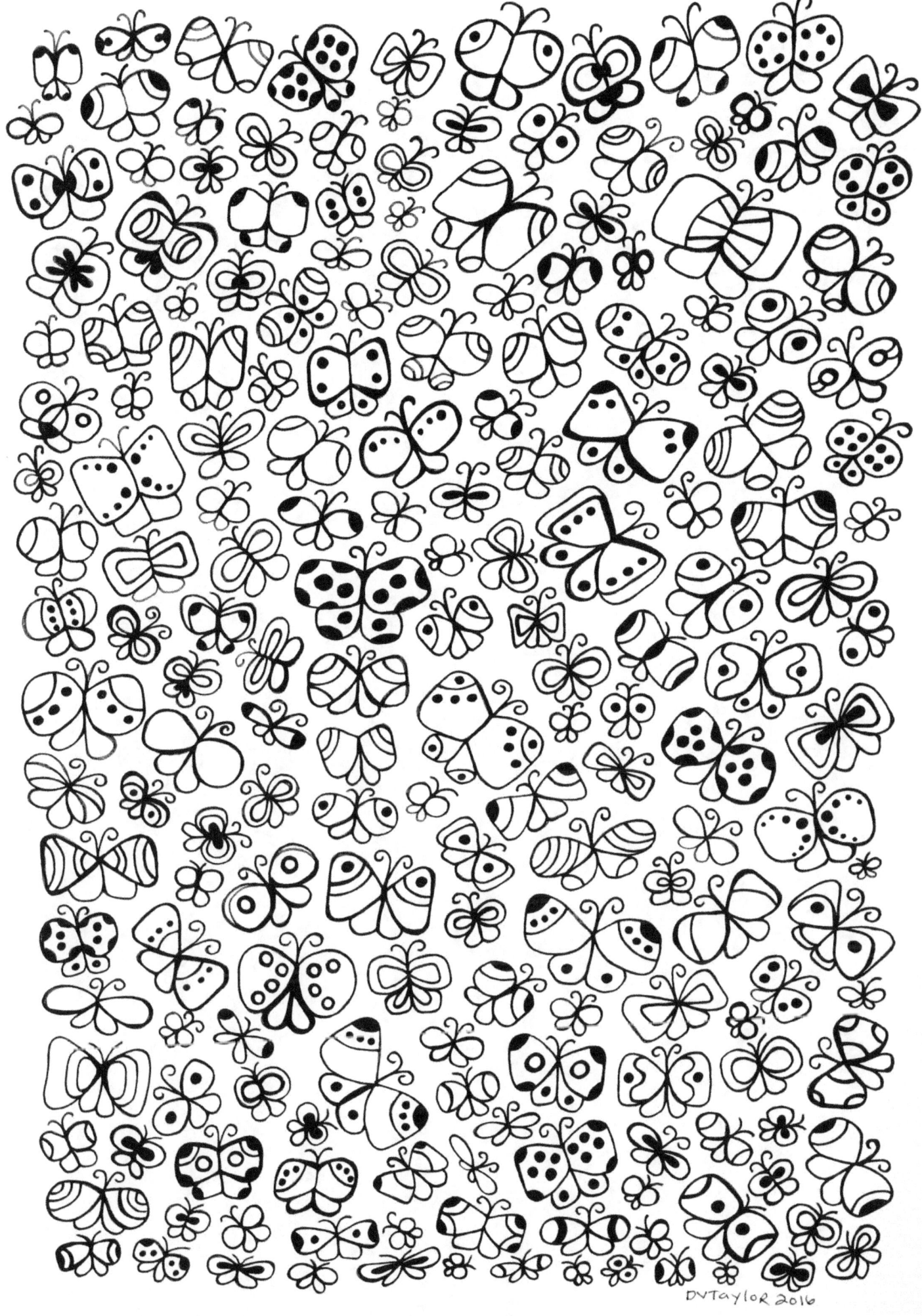

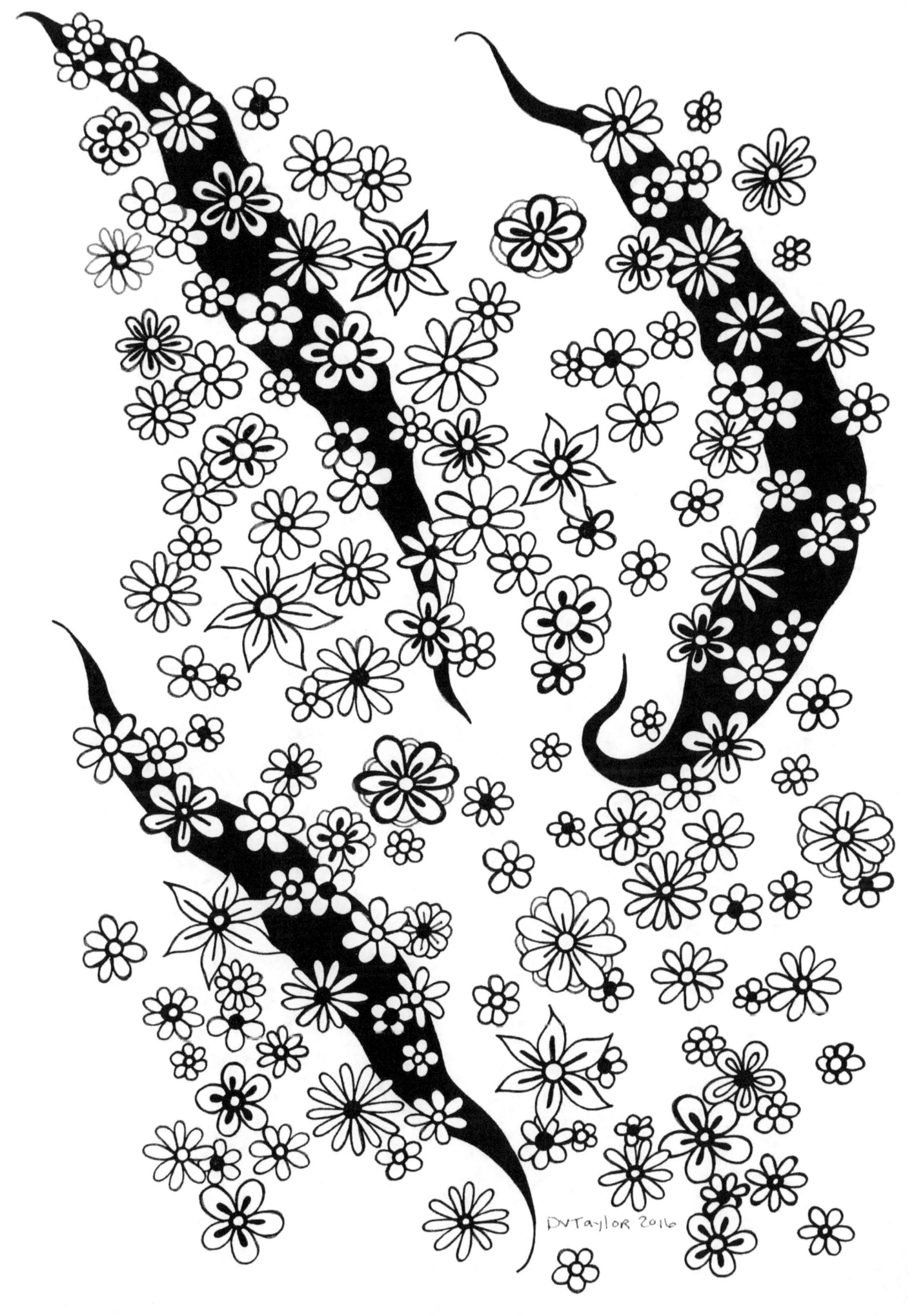

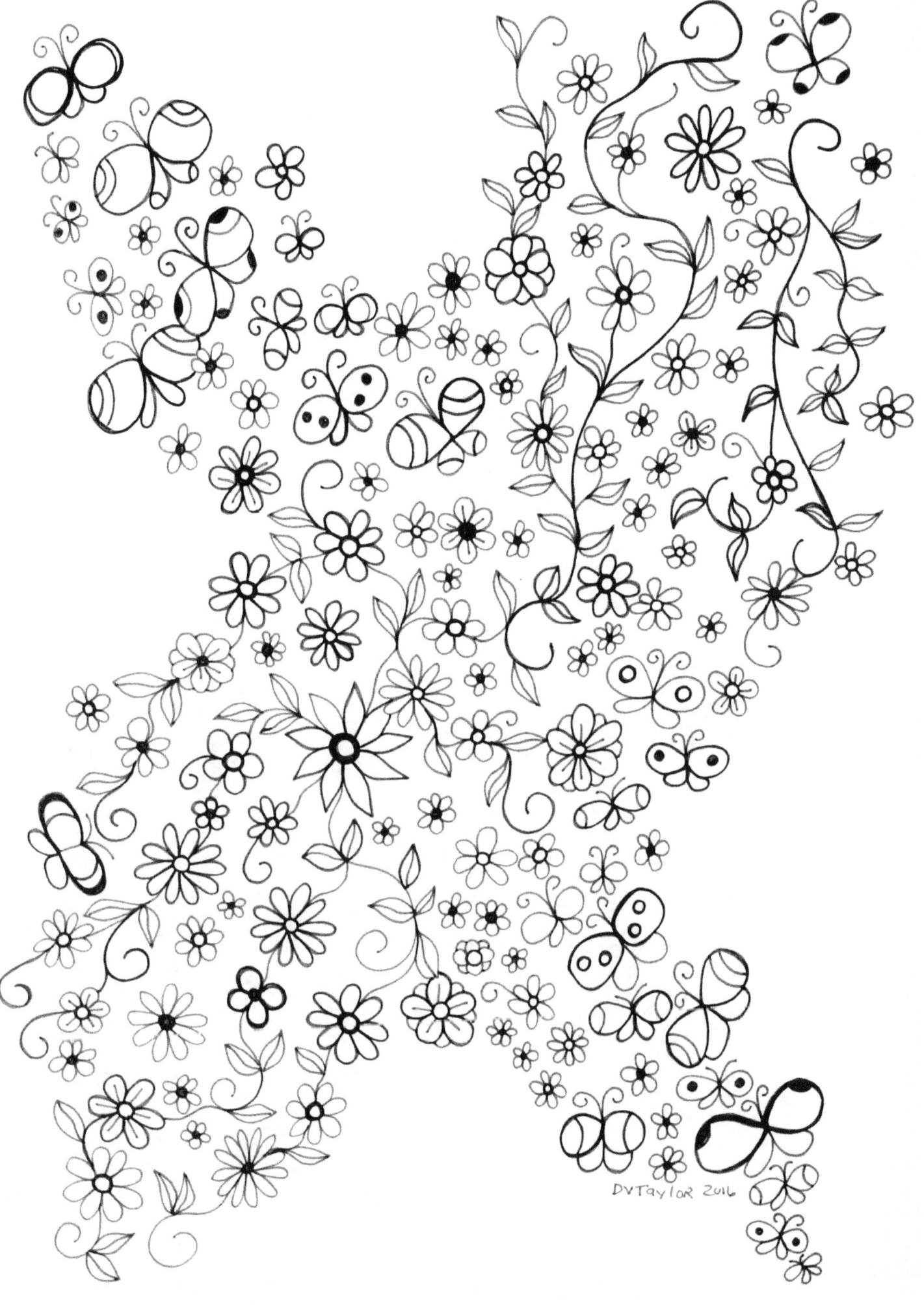

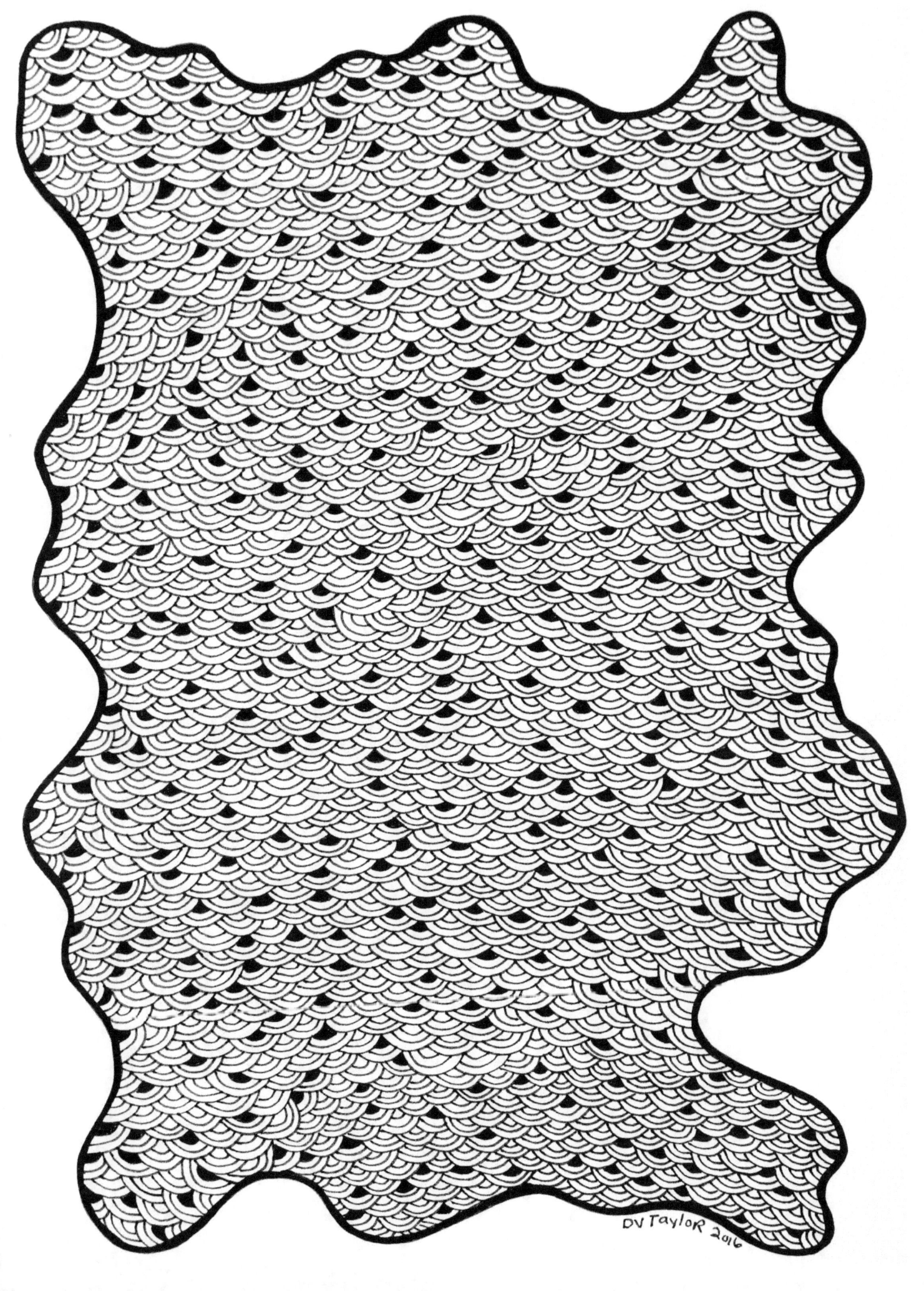

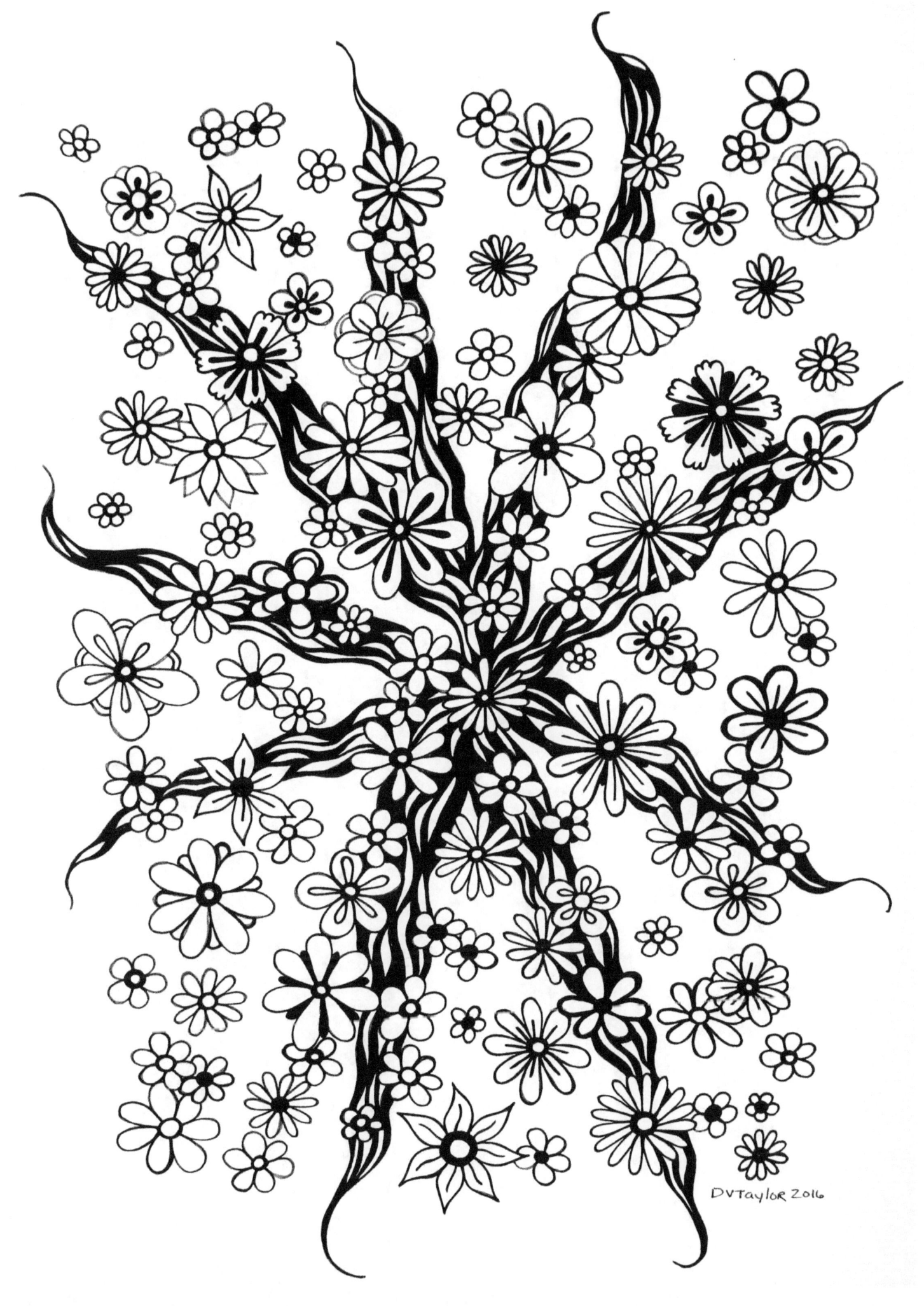

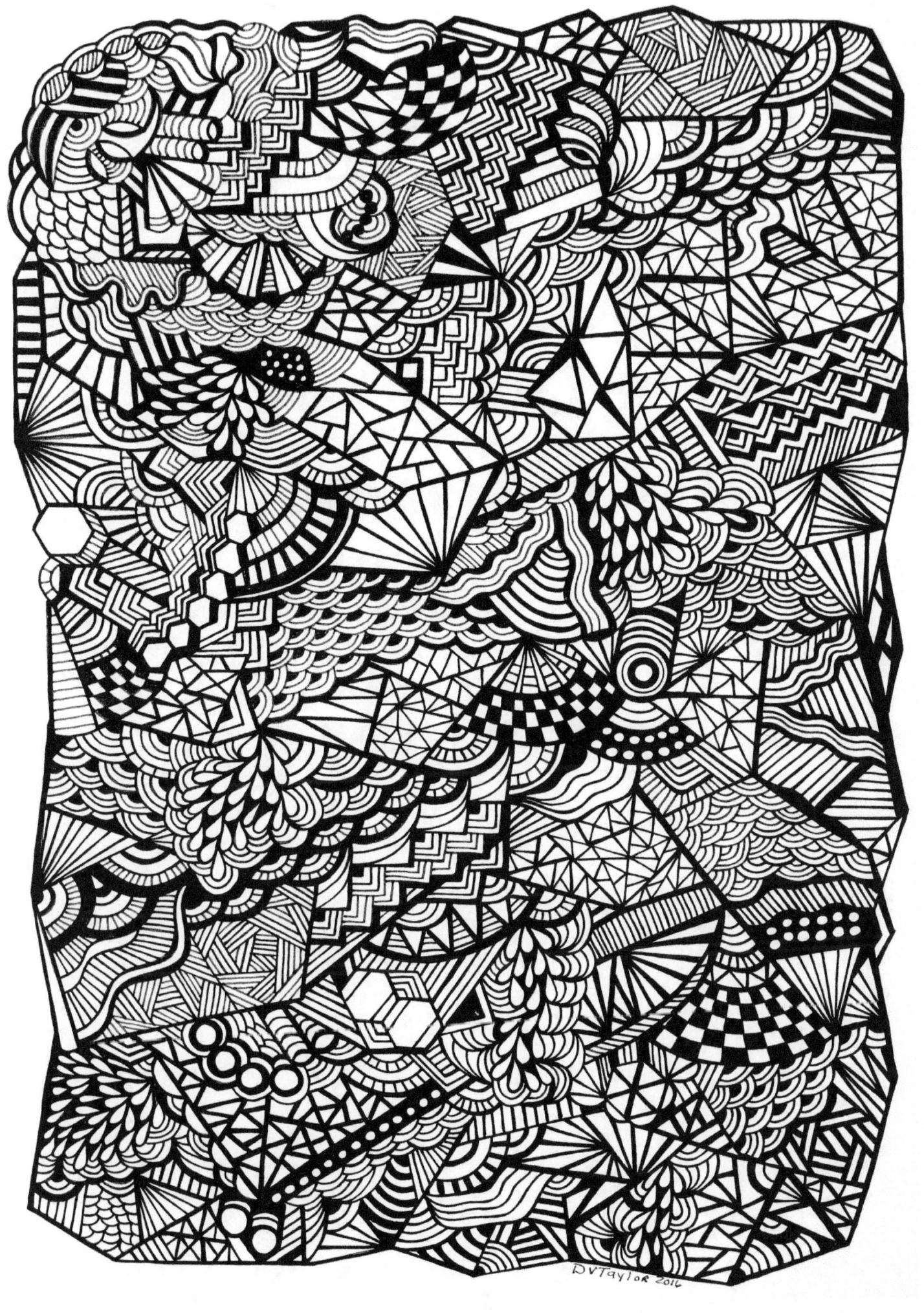

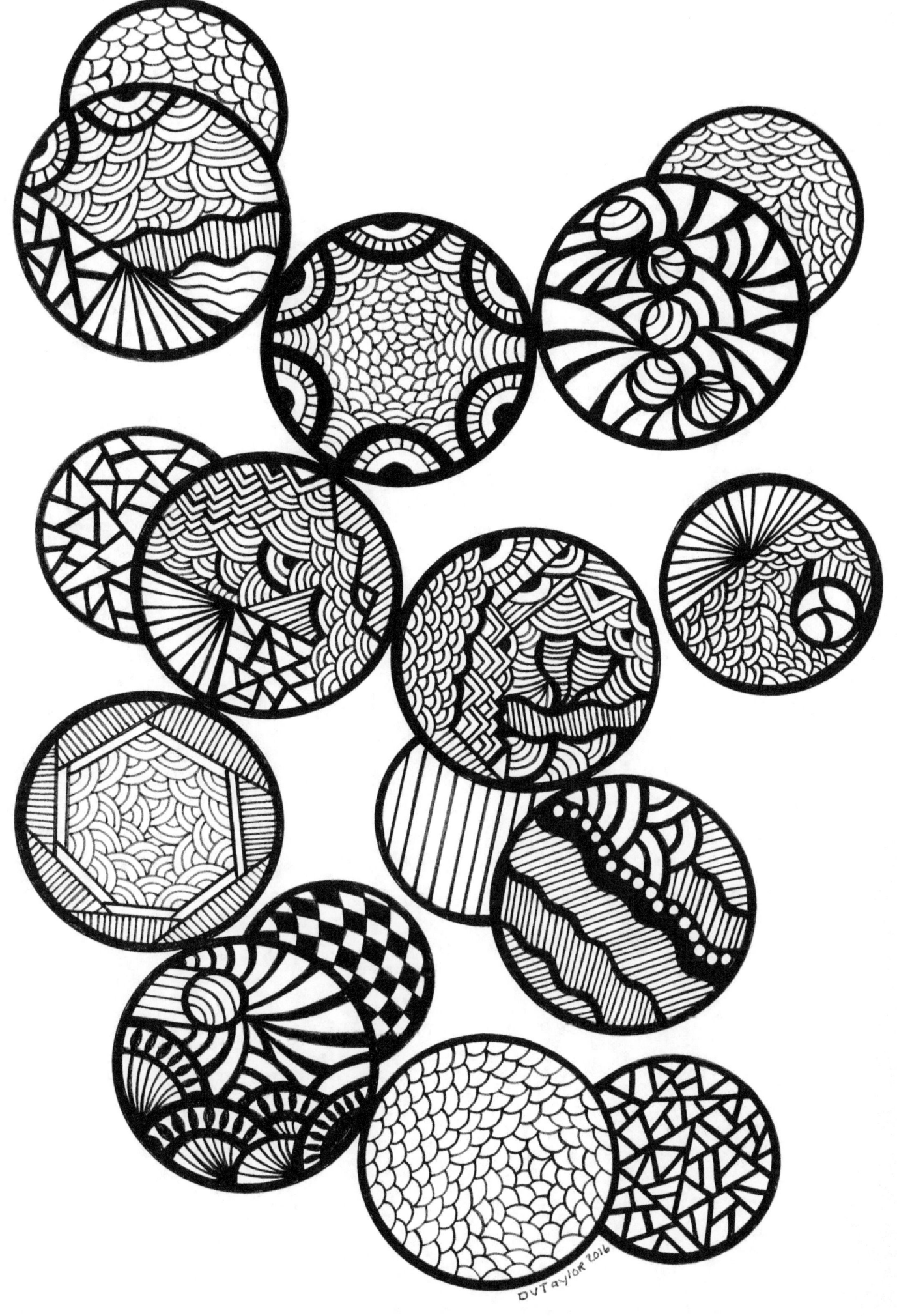

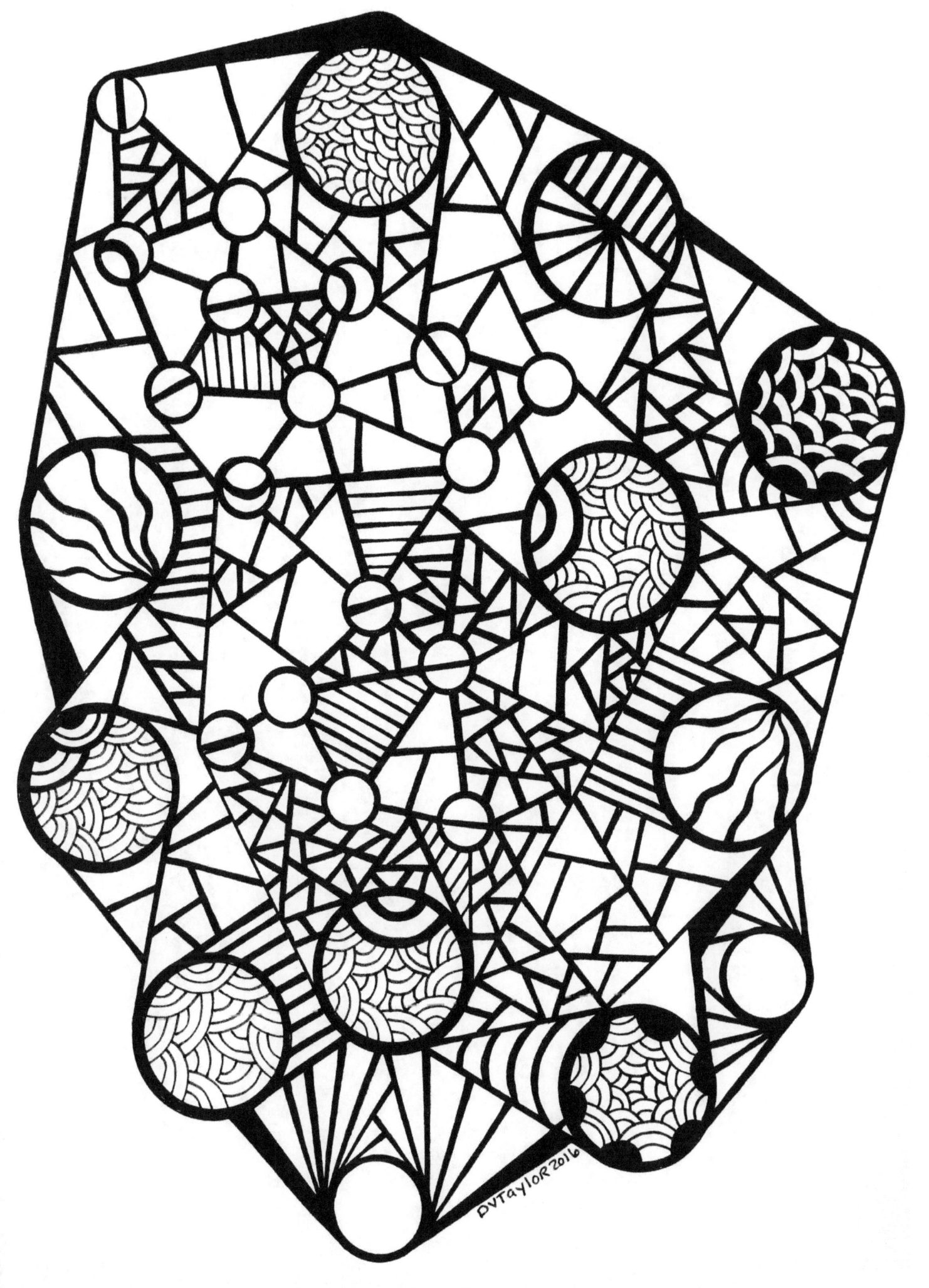

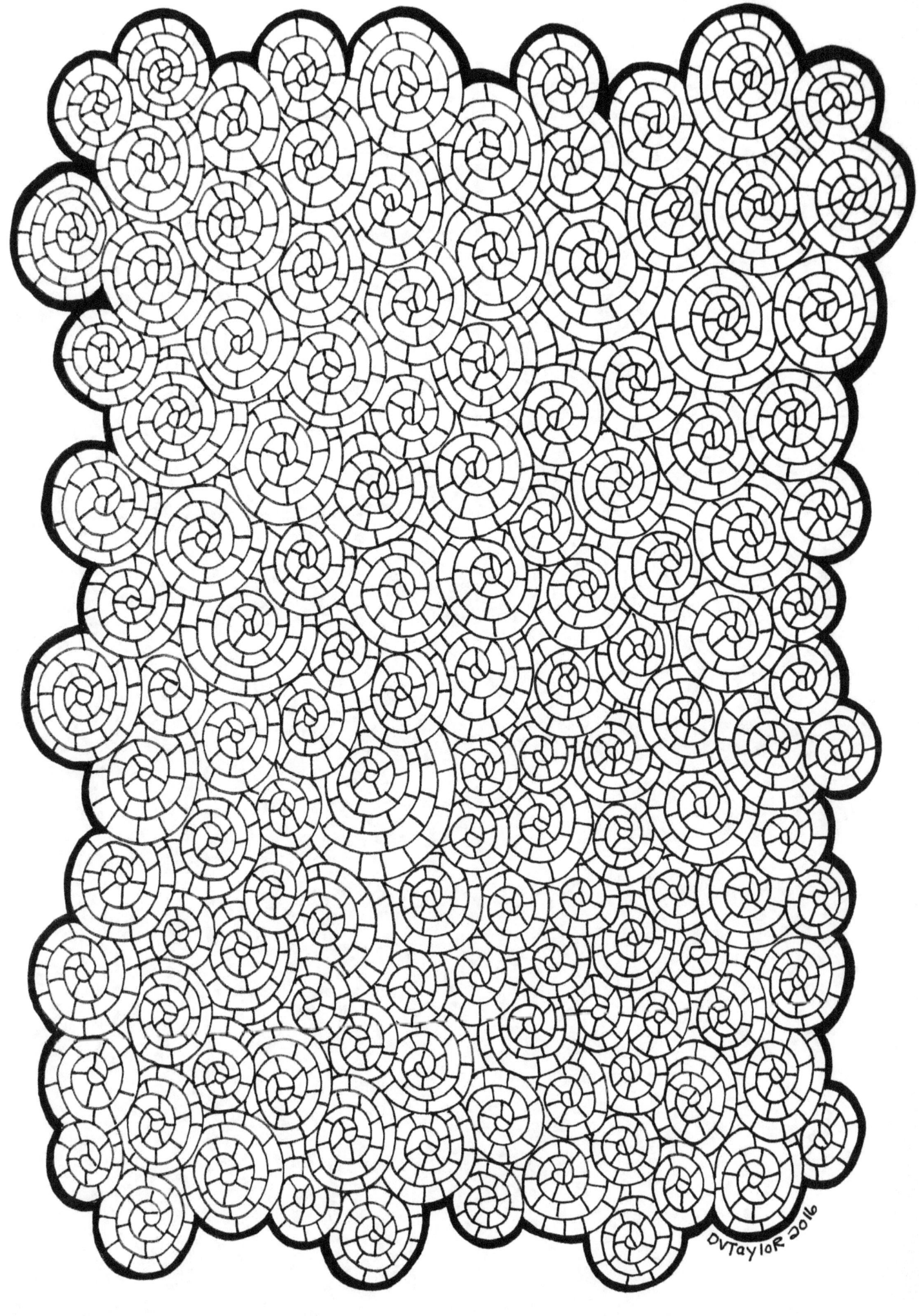

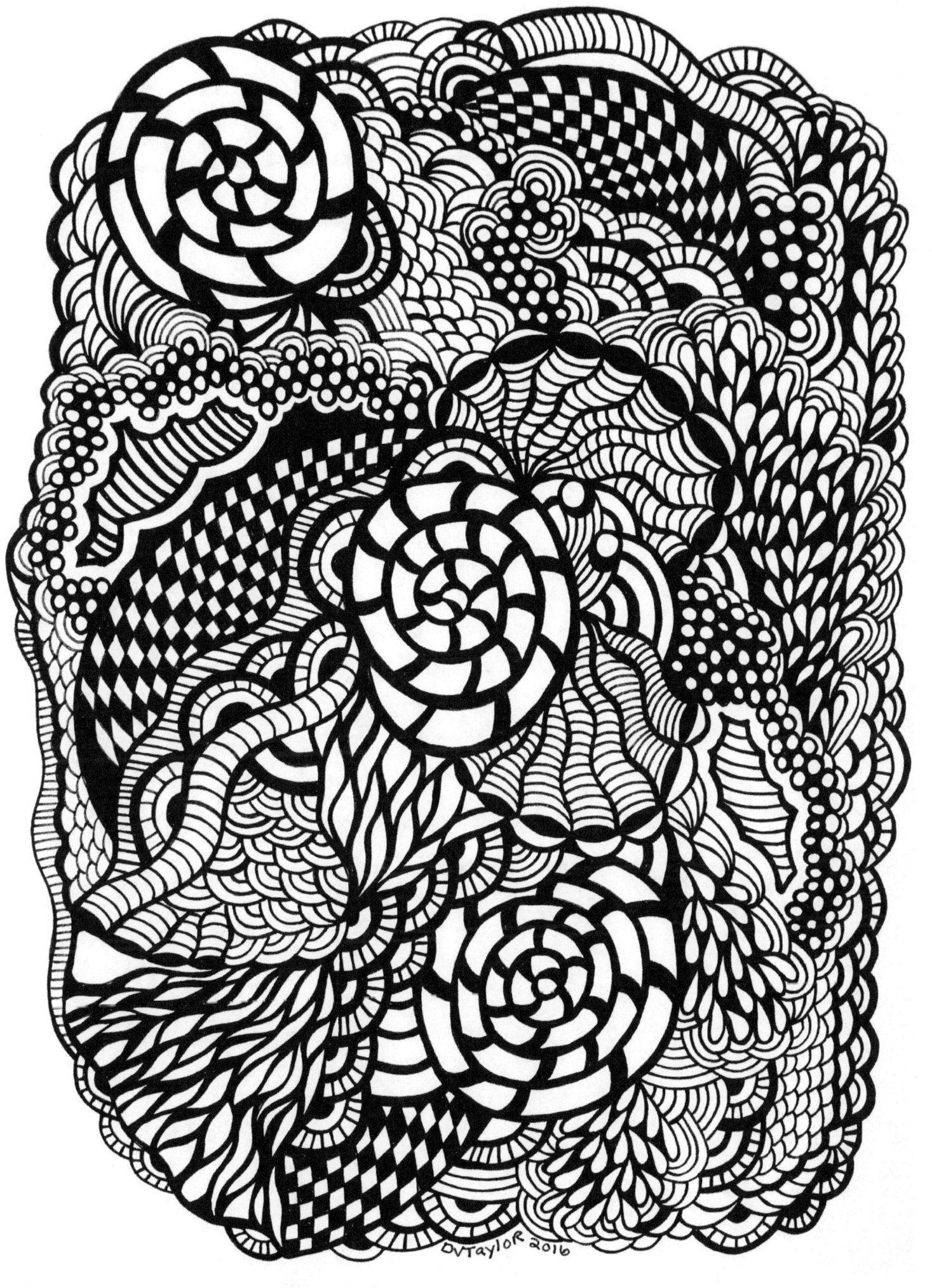

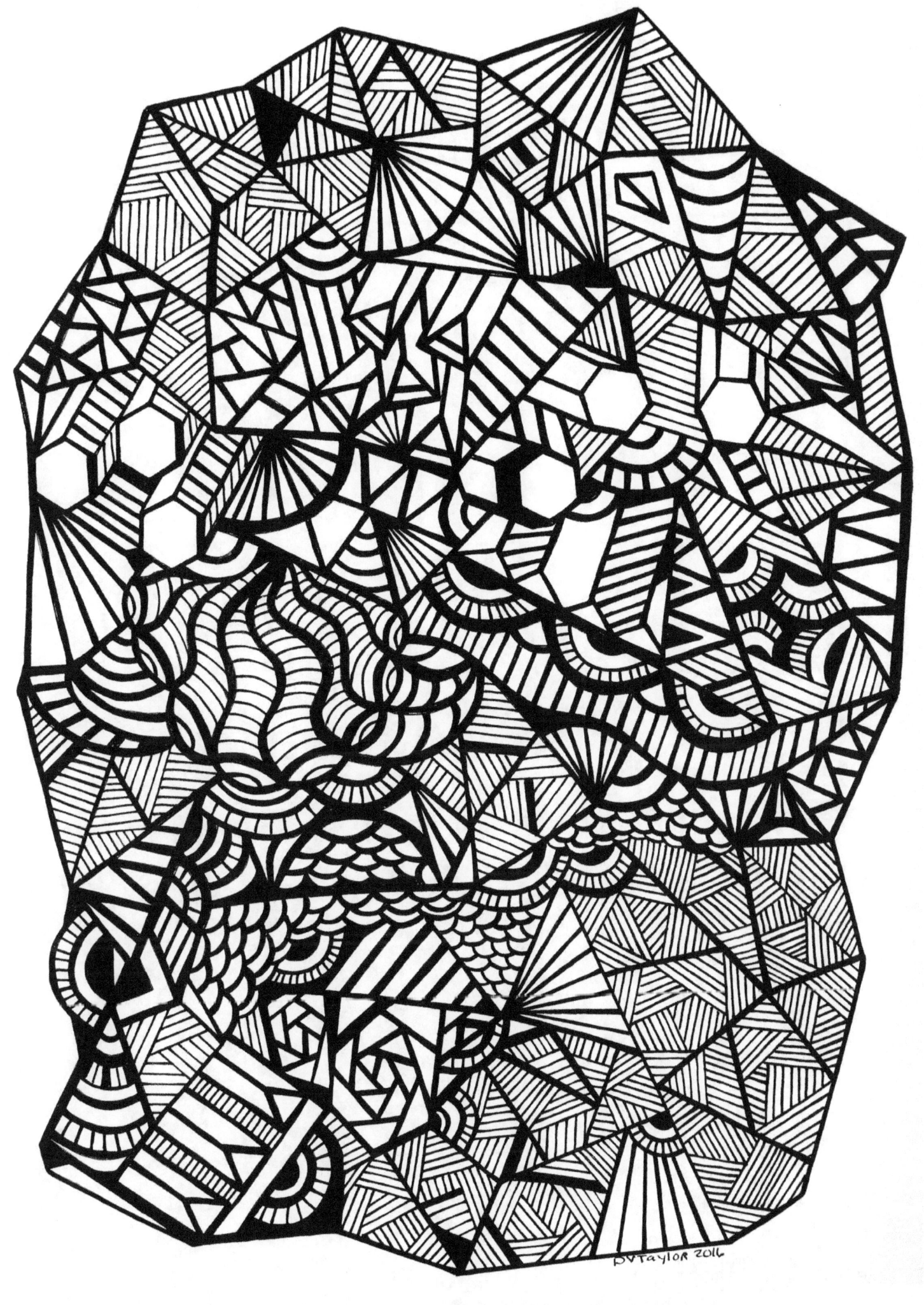